Travels with the Earth Oracle

Travels with the Earth Oracle

BOOK ONE

M. Smith

Cover photos by Karen Anderson
Illustrations by Patti Landres
Photograph on pg 23 by Jane Ball (www.janeballphotography.com);
photographs on pgs. 39, 48, 61, 110 by Karen Anderson; photographs on
pgs. 65, 83, 95, 129 by Ken Brown (www.kenwbrownphotography.com)

ISBN: 978-0-9976992-0-3

For more information about the Earth Oracle,
and the soul-body blending work of the Teacher,
go to www.theearthoracle.com.

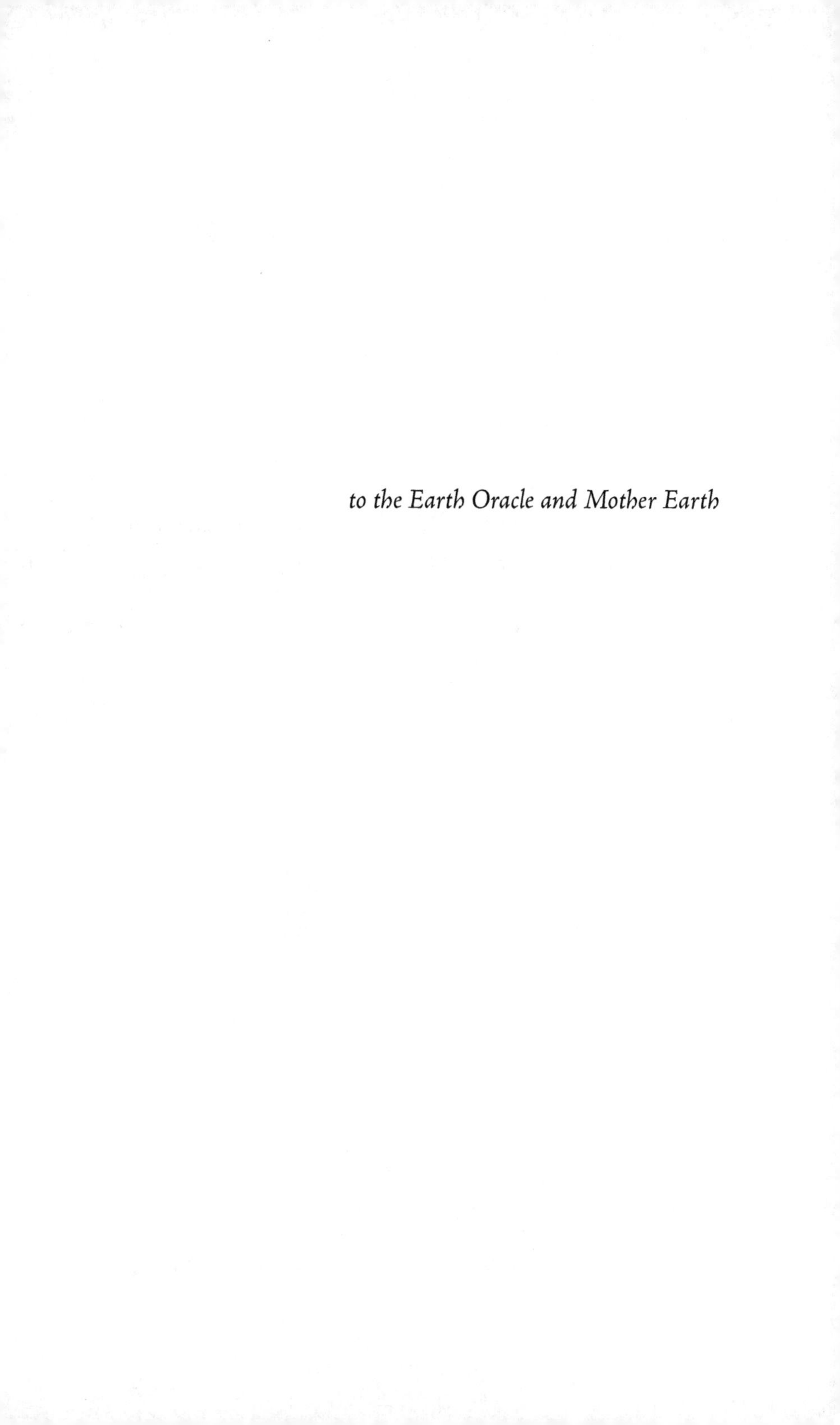

to the Earth Oracle and Mother Earth

As planetary beings your primary purpose above all others is to help sustain the Earth's balance and fortify its ability to create life.

The Teacher

Contents

Note to Readers

The quotations shown in italics were taken from transcripts of recorded trip lectures and classes. These quotes are shown as they were received; minor clarifications shown in brackets.

All quotes not cited by name are the words of the Teacher or the Master — who are two primary teachers who speak through the Oracle.

* An asterisk indicates there is more information about the topic in the Appendix at the back of the book.

(!) An exclamation point in parentheses indicates group laughter.

Introduction

This is a book of travels. Outward and inward, and most likely a departure from previous trips you've taken. The itinerary is challenging and full of surprises. Many of the guides are not of the physical world. Your fellow passengers are ordinary-looking Americans who've held jobs, paid mortgages, and raised children. The only difference is these travelers have come on board to learn how to be more conscious human beings, and becoming a conscious human being is no vacation.

Our travels, and the work involved, were directed by the Earth Oracle, a woman who carries the extraordinary ability of sensing and giving voice to a multitude of highly conscious beings, the spirit of places, and planetary life forms.

This book is a condensation of many years of study, with the focus being on specific trips we took around the world to work with the energy centers, or *chakras*, of the Earth, as well as these centers in ourselves. Being energy-based, much of the work and guided exercises we were taught and practiced are experiential in nature, making it a daunting task to articulate in tangible, sensory language.

This book does not pretend to cover the depth and scope of the information we've received and applied to our lives. What follows are snapshots lifted from a far larger panorama, a compressed version of events, much of it written through the lens of my perception and experience. This book in no way reflects or interprets the experiences of fellow travelers, whose presence and participation gave heart, community, and light to the work. My hope is this book captures the essence of the trips and honors the wisdom we received in the spirit in which it was given.

The information described here is not intended to promote, persuade, or recruit others into following the teachings, soul-body training, and Earth energy work we've undertaken. There is no single or best way to become a conscious human being. This book depicts one experimental and evolving path a number of us have walked. The spiritual work was not conducted solely by us. We were aided along the way by a number of non-physical teachers and helpers. Nothing was done to us, or for us, without our permission and our effort. It has been and remains an open-door education, with each of us being free to leave at any time and follow other pursuits.

One thing I believe my fellow travelers would agree with is that energy work with the Earth is a sacred adventure. As for the Earth Oracle, I fumble for words to describe the source of wisdom she carries. Yes, she is human like you and me, with foibles and edges, bad days, and physical limitations, but the similarities end there. She is also a mother lode of knowledge, who brings voice to an ocean of master beings, ancient sages, and conscious life forms from this and other worlds.

Preparations for Departure

As the Northwest Airlines passenger jet made its descent into the Minneapolis-St. Paul airport, I spotted a stripe of green in the sky below a bank of clouds as dark as doom. It was that ghostly green which foretells of a pending tornado. A gust of wind buffeted the wings of the 747 as the tires chaffed the tarmac. Meeting me at the gate, my wife rushed us out of the terminal in a sprint. "We've got to get home," she warned. "A big storm is coming." I wasn't panicked. This is Minnesota, the state of straight-line winds, whiteouts, black ice, and forty-degree temperature shifts within an afternoon.

We got in the door just as the storm unleashed its stampede. In no time our basement obtained a new natural feature — a gleaming waterfall gushing through the window well in a ceaseless torrent.

The night was July 23rd, 1987. A date etched in the memories of Minnesotans. Now commonly called, "the Superstorm," it brought massive flooding and destruction. The oddity of it was how the system stalled out over the Twin Cities without budging or letting up. We didn't know it at the time, but this deluge was the fanfare heralding the arrival of *the Master*, and with his appearance our travels with the Oracle would soon begin.

I use the term "oracle" in its traditional meaning — a source of spoken wisdom. In today's parlance, she would be called a "channel." More precisely, she is a physical trance medium who brings through a wide spectrum of spiritual masters and life forms capable of communicating both verbally and energetically. Being a *physical* trance medium gives her body the rare ability to radiate and move energy spatially on a vibratory level. For instance, when she talks about a place she's visited and touched, not only do the pictures from her visual memory fill the room, the energy of the place emanates from her pores.

The Oracles, the physical trance mediums, have always been typically the people that the Earth has worked through for humans. They have typically been the ones that have brought humans closer to their souls with their bodies. Other mediums, other psychics, other spiritual people, other mystics have done it in other ways. But the physical trance mediums are the ones where the bodies are included. They provided the way for you to know and acknowledge soul. The physical trance mediums not only bring in soul, but they bring in Earth soul. They have both dynamics going on.

The Teacher

Central to the treasury of beings and energies the Oracle brings through is *the Teacher*, a soul and a teacher of souls. The Teacher's primary work is to help humans develop conscious bodies in which the soul and the physical body come together as partners without either dominating or possessing the other.

The Teacher is not an angel, a protector, or a savior. He is actually a *they* — five discarnate beings who join together to teach anyone willing to work at attaining a more conscious body. He has been described as a blue mist, and to a number of students he appears visually at times as a star-bright blue dot. He treats students with acceptance and affinity — the agreement being that we are responsible for our own sovereignty, free to express our hearts and minds, and to do what we choose with the instruction.

The Teacher speaks in plain English with attention to the meaning of the words and their energetic qualities. No heady, intellectual lectures or fuzzy, other-worldly language here, but the unvarnished truth, clear, straightforward, and purposefully delivered for each student's self-realization.

The scope of the Teacher's knowledge is seemingly endless. If he doesn't have the answer to a question immediately available, he will bring in another teacher with the expertise, or he will consult *the library system*, an etheric source of universal information and wisdom.

Soul teachers, such as the Teacher who instructs us, are here to teach for a series of lifetimes, not just a single one. The information they provide may not directly pertain to this life alone but set in motion knowledge to be applied in another. It is a cycle of continuous learning. Completing the cycle of learning is achieved when you walk with it and make the information your own.

You have to wear it. It has to become part of yourself and that only happens when you use it. So that when you die you keep the information with you from one lifetime to another.

Classes with the Teacher

The Teacher's instruction and practice of soul-body integration training began with regularity in 1981 in the form of weekly classes and topic-based lectures in the western suburbs of Minneapolis.

Classes would begin with the Teacher assessing the overall energy state of the students in the room and then matching the theme of his talk to the readiness and receptivity of the group mind. There might be an entire class given to topics such as caring, everyday evil, seniority, or male passivity. The time might be spent answering students' personal questions or clarifying what unseen forces were behind current world events. The Teacher might demonstrate an unhealthy human trait by emitting its energy into the room through the Oracle's body so we could sense its particular vibration, feel where it resonated within us, or where we had experienced the energy in the world yet not consciously identified it by name.

Class content did not advance in a linear, step-by-step progression. You never knew what might be forthcoming. If anything, the spatial orchestration of the teaching and practice was circular. Information and instruction would be given to us as we were ready for it, and then later we'd return to it, taking in new knowledge as we fortified the foundation of what we'd absorbed. Much of the work was heart-based. Thinking took a back seat to feeling. There were no pass or fail grades, nor was any student ever made to feel wrong for how slow they understood or applied the information in their lives. Everyone is unique and learns in his or her own way. If one of the students needed more extensive personal attention and guidance, he or she could schedule a private session, or "reading," with the Teacher. The Oracle's calendar was booked solid a year in advance.

Although unknown to me at the time, looking back, I see how our future travels with the Oracle around the world could not have begun without receiving several years of the Teacher's instruction first. We needed to acknowledge our own dark sides, our shortcomings and unhealthy aspects to develop compassion for others. We also needed guidance and practice in stretching and strengthening our personal energy fields to connect our etheric souls[1] with our bodies in a healthier way.

1. Etheric soul: Commonly referred to as "soul," or a person's individual soul. The use of the term *etheric soul* is to distinguish it from the *human soul* described later in the book.

Soul–Body Integration

What we learned from the Teacher early on was how distant and disconnected our bodies were from our etheric souls. For those of us who believed or assumed the etheric soul came completely hardwired at birth to the physical body this revelation came as a surprise.

The reason for the disconnection is due to the amount of solidity and rigid ways of living we've carried around from our childhoods, from generation to generation, and from incarnation to incarnation. These solid aspects obstruct the blending of our etheric souls with our bodies.

Solidity can be described as non-moving energy, neither alive nor dead, in the sense of still transforming, but frozen. Types of solidity include places in us where we might hold unexpressed or unresolved traumas and wounds. It could be a way of coping as a child in a dysfunctional household that's no longer applicable or productive as an adult. It might be a lie or an imprinted belief that doesn't embrace change, diversity, or foreign ways of thinking. This frozen energy not only impedes a soul-body connection, it can also cause chronic illness, mental illness, and unhealthy patterns of behavior.

As the Oracle has pointed out, "When the connection between the body and the soul disintegrates, you can become rigidly physical with the inability to care for anything but yourself, or rigidly spiritual, in which case your beliefs are the one and only truth, and the right way for everyone."

The solidity of human beings becomes palpable when you look at the ravaged state of Mother Earth. The destruction, greed, and neglect "civilized people" inflict on the planet and each other clearly reflects the disconnected relationship between the etheric souls and physical bodies of human beings.

There is a war between bodies and souls. Where the souls wish to dominate, in many ways not listen to the body, not listen to the part of the body that knows how to live here and not destroy.

To attain and sustain an enlivened, conscious body, these solid aspects need to be named, felt, and the energy set in motion. In the early days, the Teacher placed attention on our rigid and darker parts — our unhealthy core issues, masks, ego structures, and the power levels[2] that ruled our decisions. He'd poke and prod every student, highlighting where they were cruel, frozen in fear, ungrounded, in fantasy, in judgment, in shame, blame, or guilt, out of their body, hiding, and/or merging[3] with another person.

When the group mind became sluggish or dim, the Teacher would bring in humor to help lighten up the energy in the room.

The experience of being spoken to by a discarnate being — through the body of the Oracle, whose eyes are shut — who can see and describe with crystal clarity more of your demons, self-deceptions, and intentions than you are conscious of can be intimidating, unsettling, and life-changing.

Speaking for myself, there were times I felt frisked and exposed in the high beams of the Teacher's soul sight. My games were lit up; my cons exposed; and the walls of my homemade, defensive fortress crumbling to ruins on the floor of the Oracle's den. I appreciated the Teacher's direct way of naming the demons and shortcomings of other students, just not my own. But how else could we see and feel how our solid, unhealthy parts blocked

2. Power levels: Rigid traits, beliefs, and impulses that compel and control a person's thoughts and behavior. They are very difficult for anyone to work through, and they can be carried from incarnation to incarnation.
3. Merging: This occurs when one person's identity mixes with another and both lose clarity of self. You see this in people who lack boundaries with another — they think the same, act the same, and may expect others to be like them.

the entry of our souls unless they were called out and revealed in full view of others.

Being grown adults, there was nothing to be gained by blaming parents and siblings for our unhealthy issues and stuck points. Of course, we could always argue with the Teacher's observations — he enjoys a good debate — and although I might buckle after first hearing him point something out, I found it best not to resist. Later, I could review what was highlighted with as much self-caring, kindness, and compassion as I could muster.

Consciousness comes with a very, very high price, because the price is honesty. And it means that you now have to forego your denial systems, your lies, your cover-ups, your cons, and really face whatever that truth may be. And this is a hard level to do, extraordinarily hard, for anyone. Even a master that has to face a new truth goes through the same difficulties as an unconscious person facing their first consciousness.

The Teacher's Formula for Change

The Teacher would often repeat his formula for changing unhealthy patterns of behavior, releasing stuck points, and healing emotional wounds, as well as bringing light and forgiveness to our darker parts.

His formula for change is: Acceptance, Responsibility, Control, and Change. This four-stage formula applies to whatever personal behavior, activity, or issue we seek to change in our lives. It could be a dysfunctional relationship, an addiction, or a compulsion. It could be a destructive response to a situation or a person, or a recurring, broken-record thought pattern.

ACCEPTANCE: To see and to know. This is the naming stage, when you acknowledge the problem honestly and see the truth without minimizing or exaggerating it. Acceptance needs to come with caring.*

RESPONSIBILITY: Taking personal responsibility for the problem. This is done with compassion and asking the question, "How can I begin to change this? What do I need to do to solve this problem?"

CONTROL: This step is about letting go of control in order to receive an answer to the question. This requires listening with kindness, and not trying to change or manipulate the answer you receive, but allowing the solution to come to you free of conditions.

CHANGE: Actively applying the answer to your life with forgiveness. Forgiveness allows you to make the change more fluidly without shame or guilt.

Each stage needs to be felt with the heart and the mind, otherwise the success of the change will be limited. Depending on the extent of the issue we seek to change, some of these stages might overlap or take a long time to work through.

The soul-body integration training we practiced was not limited to verbal lectures and discussion; it was also being activated energetically. The Teacher would craftily wedge openings in our walls and lift the lids off our inner coffins to allow light and energy to pass into us. It was surprising to find certain strengths and gifts we'd locked away, our personal insights and talents shielded in forgotten places in our bodies.

If you have shields up that are protecting you from your world, then you also have those shields that are keeping you outside of you. That's the price you pay for self-protection. Not only does it keep the world outside, it keeps you there, too.

Suffice it to say, there isn't a cool, breezy way of doing soul-body work with the Teacher. Self-realization is no stroll on the beach. Like creativity, it's emotionally charged and brilliantly messy. I sincerely doubt any student of the Teacher would claim they've had a pleasant time of it. Certainly the Teacher never promised us a joy ride or instant happiness. "Follow your bliss" is not one of the Teacher's mottos. Given the solidity in our bodies and minds, he often noted how the work would be painful.

This is by far the most grueling, the most painful, most rejoiceful thing you can ever do.

Physical Bodies and Etheric Souls

Souls and bodies have strikingly different natures. The subtle, etheric energy of the soul moves along at a higher vibratory rate than physical energy. It has been described as "light without shadows," and it shines its light on our dark, unconscious places as well as our strengths and weaknesses.

The etheric soul seeks change, it seeks expansion — to create beyond one's self. But as we work to breathe more of our etheric soul into our body, we have no control over what it will illuminate, or when.

Many people don't want to work with their souls because when the soul hits a place that the body does not want to change, the soul becomes the enemy.

Through the Teacher's instruction, we learned how the etheric soul is not a pure, heavenly angel, as some surmise. Nor is the physical body a primal, inferior organic form that is here to serve as a vehicle for the soul's entertainment. The body is a wondrous instrument that allows the formless nature of the etheric soul to experience the multi-dimensions* of physical life in an Earthly form. However, just as the soul's presence provides knowledge of the etheric realm, it can be harmed by the trauma experienced in its physical lives. If not fully healed between lives, the soul can carry these wounds from incarnation to incarnation.

Some wounds and dark areas cannot be healed in one lifetime. One works toward understanding what is behind the wound or darkness, becoming conscious of the emotions around it. Wisdom in action is showing compassion for others with similar issues.

The goal is to bring the etheric soul and physical body together as partners where neither fears nor overpowers the other.

The prayer of the soul is that of creation; the prayer of the body is that of development. Freedom is the two together being one. [When] the two come together, they create the third. Let not the soul possess the body and let not the body possess the soul. They are peers, they are not equal. They are separate and different. Keep them unique.

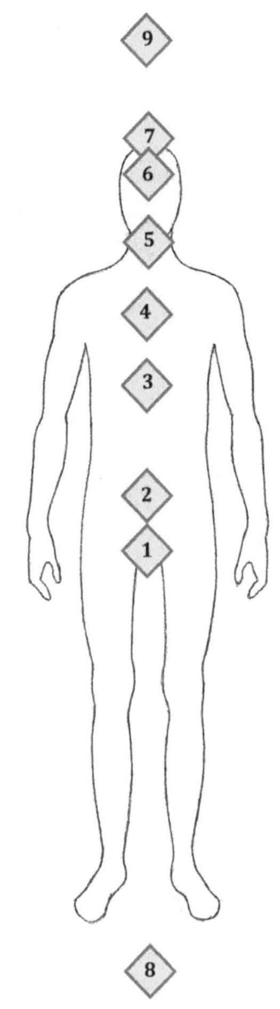

The Energy Body

A vital part in developing a healthy soul and body union is working to open, strengthen, and expand our personal energy field. This includes the spiritual anatomy of the human body, which guides, monitors, and exchanges energy with our physical anatomy and with the world.

Some of the centers in the energy body are well known, such as the chakras, others less so. There are many books on the human spiritual anatomy and many teachers who espouse the seven-chakra system.* During our soul-body training, it was essential for us to include the eighth and ninth chakras.

This graphic illustrates the nine-chakra system of the human spiritual anatomy.

The eighth chakra, or *Earth chakra,* is located below the feet. It is the center through which all energies of the Earth enter the physical body.

The ninth chakra is the gateway for the soul. It is an etheric center located above the head, and it functions as a filter for the entry of universal information and etheric energy into the body.

More structures of the human spiritual anatomy will be revealed later in this book, as they were introduced and integrated into our soul work.

Running Energy

"Running our energy" was an ongoing activity to help us bring in more of our etheric soul. This involved intentionally applying motion and direction to the personal energy field radiating around our bodies. We'd move the energy into the Earth below our feet to help us be more grounded, in present time, and behind our eyes.

The present has to become more important than the past if one is to actually begin to walk one's path.

We also needed to pay particular attention to our breathing, keeping our hearts open, removing mental chatter, and being mindful not to judge what was being highlighted in ourselves and others.

Running energy is an insightful tool for self-realization. It heightens awareness of your current state of being — where your energy is flowing and where it's bottled up, contracted, moving erratically, or dominating a particular chakra. Our energy bodies are always talking whether we're conscious of them or not. Running energy helps us be more mindful and honest about ourselves, to name and accept who we are and where we are at, and make choices to bring balance, healing, and strength* to our lives.

In time, running energy became an essential part of our classes. We'd stand with our hands at our sides as the Teacher guided us along, pointing out areas in us where the energy was stagnant or imbalanced. He'd have us look at the difference between what we were saying and the energy our bodies were emitting, and he would ask, "Which is true? Which is a lie?" Over time, we became more aware of the character of our personal energy field — a field that requires continuous tending in order to gain and sustain an enlivened, conscious body.

Anyone expecting an instant lightning bolt of cosmic consciousness while doing the Teacher's soul work would be disappointed. You'd also be fooling yourself to think the work would remove all fear, doubt, sickness, and chronic pain, make you rich or thin, or set you floating on a sea of emotional calm. Having a conscious body does not protect you from the world or dissolve your problems away. However, the more conscious you become the more alive you feel, the more sensitive you are to the outside world, and the more choices available for you to reach for health and seek solutions.

It should never hurt you to bring in [your] soul. It should only be difficult for the struggle of preparing the soul and body to be together. But once together, it is natural, amazingly natural. So, it's very much all in the effort of the preparation.

After six years of continuous weekly study, it was clear we were engaged in a spiritual work-in-progress with a source of ever-unfolding instruction on how to blend our souls and bodies in a harmonious way.

The Master's Grand Entrance

Along came a class in July 1987.

The Oracle sat in a tall-backed chair with a semicircle of about twenty students facing her. We were all abuzz with talk of the Superstorm that had just flooded the metro area. The Oracle went into trance and, to our surprise, her body suddenly bolted up out of her chair.

Instead of the Teacher, who never stood up, we were greeted with a burst of exhalation from a high-energy being who exalted, "I am the Master! Did you like my rain?"

Spiritually speaking, the term "master" conjures up pictures of a wise, serene, and humble person who has reached a high state of consciousness and inner peace. Yet the one strutting around the room in all his energetic glory was anything but the embodiment of tranquility. This master carried the spirit of the planet Uranus — explosive, expansive, and exuberant.

"What took you sooo long." He theatrically feigned a wearied, pained look. "I've been waiting and waiting for, oh, I can't count how many of your years!"

Seeing a different being was not new to us. The Teacher's way of instruction often brought out other beings and energies for us to experience, many of them unsavory, some even terrifying. But the Master was a quantum jump from any of them, and he knew it. He joked how the Teacher was blue, whereas he was gold. How the Teacher was "stuffy," whereas he was "magnificent."

As the Oracle once pointed out to me, "Souls and master beings are unique. They're not saintly, or perfect, or precious, and their teaching methods can vary dramatically."

The Master was clear about his method:

My purpose is not to teach you. It's to open you up.

And open us up he did. In forthcoming classes, the Master would start by going around to the men in the room and beating on their chests. Once he had their hearts tenderized and thumping, he'd move to the women and stretch their limbs, arch their backs, twist their necks, anything to get energy moving. He'd pull the "dead things" off of us — glasses, hats, scarves, and coats — so he could work more directly on our bodies. He'd crack jokes about the energy we were running, or the lack thereof, or mimic a student's present state with theatrical exaggeration to spark laughter at ourselves. Humor moves energy, and if ever there was a mover and shaker of energy, it is the Master.

Most striking, with the Master's appearance there was a tectonic shift in our soul-body work. No longer did the instruction center solely on our self-realization. It now became more about the Earth, a planet in crisis, and our need to help reawaken its energy centers, which had been closed down long ago to safeguard its life force from extermination.

The following historical account sounds like the opening hook of a science fiction novel. Yet having been given so much straight truth and wisdom over the years from the Teacher, and now the Master, it would be a disservice to dismiss it outright.

The Closing

Thousands upon thousands of years ago[4] there lived on Earth human beings who saw it necessary to put the soul of the planet into a dormant, sleep-like state by closing down its chakras. This undertaking was only achieved with its consent.

---

4. A soul's perception of physical timing is not exact. Students would often ask the Teacher to pinpoint when an event happened or will take place, only to receive a non-specific number, in this case, "thousands upon thousands of years."

The Earth was different then, with a different configuration of continents. Antarctica did not have snow.

It was a time when a growing wave of darkness had entered the planet bringing with it increasing destruction. The earthly harmony was cracking apart as people sought dominance over nature, and each other — killing creatures with no need or intention of eating them and ruthlessly taking for themselves without giving back. Thinking became more rigid, controlling, and narcissistic, separating people because of their personal beliefs, and causing conflict, war, and enslavement.

"That's how it started," the Oracle explained. "When we learned we could hurt each other and normalized it, that's when darkness began on this planet."

The planet was created to be a jewel in the darkness. The jewel tarnished because evil sneaked in.

Gradually, the light and fluid nature of the etheric world was receding, and the soul and body connection was being diminished and replaced by a growing fearfulness and contraction. For many, Mother Earth was no longer perceived as a living, conscious being who created and nurtured a multitude of interdependent life forms. Instead, it had become a resource to be mined, possessed, and devoured.

The more conscious ones sensed how the tone of the Earth was changing; its vibratory qualities and vitality were lessening. They also saw how their etheric soul connection was being forgotten in exchange for a false truth, a truth that placed God outside of them, a truth that said the only reality was the physical world and this is all there is. Their bodies would eventually die, and with death there would be nothing more.

By believing the physical world was the only reality, they shut off the light of their inside world, and in doing so, they lost the insight, the caring, and the deeper range of consciousness that comes with an intimate connection with self and with the soul of the planet.

Solidity was setting in, and the conscious ones — those who could still connect with the heart and soul of the Earth — willingly took it upon themselves to travel great distances around the world and close down the planet's chakras, putting them into a state of hibernation to prevent the Earth's life force from being irretrievably damaged and all its knowledge forgotten.

These were a unique set of people. There were not many at that time who had the consciousness to understand that the Earth is a living being whose life force was being destroyed by the murder. They understood their soul's karma was embedded with the Earth's karma. If the chakras were not put into a state of hibernation, the planet would go down with all the killing and destruction being inflicted. If it was murdered, their souls would be greatly impacted by it.

The Closing would not stop the rampant destruction, but it would limit it to the surface, sparing much of the planet's core and its soul. Once completed, no one could penetrate these energy centers without permission from the Earth and knowledge of the equations that sealed and secured all access — an energy code, if you will.

The reason human beings needed to put the planet's chakras into hibernation and not the Earth, itself, was because humans were perpetrating the harm.

Nature says the same species that does the destruction must bring the balancing.

The human body is a mirror of the planet, and the conscious ones knew closing the Earth's chakras would dramatically limit the connection they had with their own etheric souls and higher selves. A part of each soul would become encased in the solidity of the body, and in this solid state they would murder and enslave each other, much like the others around them, enacting harm and enduring tremendous cruelty and pain for lifetimes to come.

They knew they'd be entrapped but not be trapped completely. At some point and some time, they would be able to re-gather and bring it back.

At each chakra closing, the conscious ones gave a personal attribute or strength of themselves to the planet for safekeeping. They gave this part freely, hoping at some point in the far distant future they might return to retrieve it — when the time came to reopen the Earth's chakras and reawaken its soul.

It's a fascinating story. One that begs the question: Why awaken the Earth's chakras at this point in time? Given the blight of wars and genocide, the stripping of great forests, poisoning of waters, toxic contamination of the air and extinction of species, surely the times are darker now than eons ago when the Earth's chakras were put to sleep. Opening them now would be like Sleeping Beauty waking up and finding her body had been brutalized while she slumbered.

The answer is in the timing. Our solar system is currently traversing through the galactic center, the Milky Way's birthplace of stars. With this rebirthing, the Earth needs to come fully awake for its soul to open into a new cycle, a new age — an age that might see the extinction of the human species.

The Master proposed to us the unusual task of helping to reawaken these sleeping chakra centers of the planet, and in the process more fully open these energy centers in our bodies. The undertaking could not be done remotely, or psychically, through mental imaging or prayer. Our souls might know the spirit of a place etherically, but the body has to know it by touching it physically. So, we needed to be at these sites with our feet on the land in order to help open, heal, and be touched in as much completeness as we could give and receive.

Talk about a high and mighty proposition! On the surface, it sounds like a ridiculously audacious endeavor, yet it was not delivered as a rousing "save the world" motivational speech, but more as a necessary activity, a functional Earthbound purpose that resonated in our hearts and minds as a natural extension of our soul-body training.

Agreement was unanimous, even though we were not aware at the time where in the world we'd be going and the work involved — travels that would help us more fully understand how we became prisoners of solidity and the scope of the destruction it has caused. Travels that would test our commitment, arouse the karmic pain of our detachment from Mother Earth, stretch us physically and spiritually, and reveal a depth of consciousness long lost.

Cathedral Rock, Sedona

The American Southwest

You cannot bring energies to these chakras, open them up, or bring any level of consciousness to them, or work with them without impact and transformation actually occurring for your outside world and your inside world simultaneously.

In November 1987, fifty-one students of the Teacher assembled with the Oracle in northern Arizona to help awaken the first chakra of the Earth, the root chakra of survival. Although our work was localized to the Sedona area, the first chakra covers a large patch of the American Southwest, including the Grand Canyon, Monument Valley, the Colorado River system, and the atmosphere of the region. Before the advent of the automobile, this arid, austere, and otherworldly landscape was certainly a place where a person's survival would be challenged; it's an unforgiving habitat for the weak of heart, body, and will.

This region has become an international magnet for new age tourists and mystical explorers. For many, the draw to Sedona has been to experience the energies emanating from its vortexes, as well as take in the magnificent russet and buff sandstone rock formations jutting like castles from the high desert terrain.

All the sites in and around Sedona for conducting our energy work had been selected by the Teacher in advance of our arrival, with astronomical alignments playing a prominent role in the timing of this and subsequent trips.

We started with a hike up Boynton Canyon, where we circled around the Oracle with rain pouring down on us, popping on our ponchos and improvised raincoats tailored out of trash bags. The Master informed us that we were a special group, but not to get arrogant about it because there were many other special groups working in similar ways to help wake up the planet.

The Oracle shared later, "No group is so special that they don't have to work hard to awaken a giant. It requires more caring than ability. Caring that goes beyond love and joins with life in such a way that not only can you begin to see more clearly, more consciously, but you also touch one of the deepest places of knowledge."

Our work at each site involved actively being in our healthiest space as best we could — without fear, arrogance, or being in a victim state — and running energy in a connective way with each other and with the Earth. We came to serve as living conduits, directing the etheric energy of our souls through our feet in order to engage with the planet's energy at each spot. The Oracle's body served as the primary battery for the energies needed to open the first chakra.

Alice

Prior to the trip, the Teacher and the Master spoke of forces that would try to stop us from fulfilling the energy work we had traveled there to accomplish. These forces would come from the outside world as well as from within ourselves. Rather than use the word "evil," which carries fear-inducing connotations, they called it "Alice," which took away some of the charge and allowed us to talk about evil with a smile, or at least less reaction.

In the Teacher's classes, we'd come to understand evil's range of destructive characteristics, both outward and subliminal, from "pure evil," which enjoys perpetrating harm repeatedly without remorse, to the "everyday evil" we carry. This is evil that knowingly or unconsciously undermines, isolates, confuses, controls, and manipulates others, subtly preying on another's vulnerabilities. Although none of us carried pure evil, we needed to be vigilant in not allowing the everyday variety to fracture us as a group and weaken our ability to complete the work.

It is very important that you understand the fight you have. Alice will do everything to make sure there is no unity and that you don't want to bond together and stay together.

Four men were picked to stand like sentries outside the group circle to help deflect Alice's alienating influence. Those circling around the Oracle were to sustain a connection with each other. If anyone became weak or imbalanced, they were reminded to ask for help or step out of the circle.

It's okay to be fragile and vulnerable. Name it. Be honest with it. You can be tired and still connect. Alice will do its best to make you even more tired and feel like you shouldn't be vulnerable, that the group is wrong, or your tiredness is wrong. You are feeling the Earth's grief and its fragileness now.

Besides Boynton Canyon, the first chakra work in Sedona took us to the Airport Vortex, Courthouse Rock, Bell Rock, and Cathedral Rock. The physical exertion of hiking to these sites was an essential part of the work. Not only were we stretching our muscles as we put our attention on staying connected as a group, we were also walking the energy of the land into our bodies so that when we reached the intended spot we'd be more grounded and more in touch with the spirit of the place.

At many of the sites we visited, the Master shared specific planetary laws. He'd step around within the circle tapping the points of a quartz crystal in his hands, urging us to not only hear the laws, but to invite the spirit of them deep into the cells of our bodies.

There are laws on this planet that pertain to all, and that you must live by. Most of these laws have been broken. And many of you have broken these laws, not intentionally, some of you knowingly, some unknowingly. Your society almost forces you to break [these] laws at some level.

Law of Survival

Being the first chakra of the Earth, it came as no surprise that "Survival of the Fittest" would be the first law we were given.

Survival of the fittest doesn't mean that you must always be fit. It doesn't make might right. You know the strength of a mind can outdo the strength of a muscle. It means sometimes in your life you will no longer be fit. And that is the time to let go, and as you find yourselves getting ready to die, you might be able to let your body go back to the planet.

We were told how in the years to come we would need to be very strong. The planet would be going through rocky, dark times, and it would need its strength to survive — and we would need ours. This was not news to us. The Teacher had been forecasting future upheavals in classes for years, even suggesting how mankind would more likely go out with a bug than a bomb.

One of the reasons the Earth would be going though such dire times was due to the unending neglect and barbaric abuse inflicted by humankind — raping the resources the Earth needs to sustain its balance and vitality, poisoning its waters, reducing oxygen levels, and exterminating species. By extinguishing the sounds of species, the planet's ability to create new life forms is severely handicapped.* Today we're seeing the boomerang effect of our destructive ways.

Law of Giving Back to the Planet

The land that you're standing on says to you most clearly,
"What I am is precious. You must give back what I give to you."

The Master made it clear how critical it is for humans to replenish the Earth so it can keep giving. He taught us the Earth is not a bottomless pit with infinite resources for the taking.

The planet has always provided for every living species. When there has been a drought, the species have been able to move and go where there is abundance. When there have been changes, the species have been able to move with those changes. It is man that has made the limitations. And it is man that has upset nature. Nature has always provided. Be one with nature and know you are provided for. Know that there's always substance for you. And understand how you must reach out and use it in all its completeness. Without waste. Know it with all your lives and with all the generations to come.

We don't need to look any further than the Native Americans to find a tangible example of utilizing Earthly creation in "all its completeness." The Plains Indians honored and repurposed every part of the buffalo. In addition to obtaining nourishment from its meat, the animal supplied them with clothing, utensils, and decorations from its hide, horns, hooves, tail, sinew, and fur. They even used dry buffalo poop for fuel.

One way of giving back to the planet today is by protecting wilderness areas and creating and sustaining life-bearing spaces that provide sustenance and habitat for native wildlife — trees, vegetation, mammals, birds, and pollinators. This activity might have little to do directly with feeding our stomachs, like planting an apple orchard or a cornfield, but it has everything to do with feeding and replenishing the cycles of life on Earth.

Law of Being Caretakers

Later, gathering at Bell Rock, the Master shared one of the major laws given to humankind: We are caretakers of the planet.

You are touching a tremendous responsibility. Be very careful. The basic law is that you are caretakers. Your responsibility is that you allow this planet to live and you help its life forms. And yet man has made its life forms extinct and now man is trying to make this planet extinct.

You have a fight on your hands. So now fight for the continuum.[5] *And fight for all that you are. If you know all that you are, and who you are, you won't be so busy controlling others and telling others what to do.*

The planetary laws he shared felt like common sense. Harking back to the story of the people who put the chakras of the Earth to sleep eons ago, it's easy to understand how the devastation of the land and waters started. By becoming more and more disconnected we'd lost our purpose as guardians of the very source that gives us life.

What is surprising is how the spirit of these laws somehow survived in the hearts and beliefs of native, pre-conquest cultures, who were once perceived as savages, and who are still viewed today as inferior. Had the world fully adopted their views, perhaps

5. Continuum: The continuous interplay of life and death in which new creation evolves from the knowledge it is fed by the dying.

humanity would not have come to such a dire impasse. Special forces might have been organized to patrol the lands and seas of the Earth, arresting any and all planetary law-breakers. Imagine an international court being established to enforce crimes against nature, viewing them as no different from violent crimes committed by one person against another.

Medicine Wheels

At one site, we came upon a number of medicine wheels on the ground made of stones. The Master came in and explained how there should be only one major medicine wheel at each location to best encompass the energy. Circles of stones can be set within the main medicine wheel, but having a number of wheels side by side diminishes the strength of them all.

The Battery

Wherever we went around the Sedona region, the Oracle's body acted like a fully-charged battery, sending a surge of energy into the land to help awaken the Earth's first chakra. The combined energy the group emitted was a small fraction of the energy radiating from her body.

Being a battery is both exhilarating and exhausting. The Oracle feels a heightened awareness; her senses sharpen, allowing her to see and hear things beyond normal perception. "There's an untold amount of energy in my body besides me," she explained. "I can go and go, hiking forever in a semi-trance state. I'm able to charge up everyone's energy, which helps do the work. But after a deep trance, I'm a deflated balloon."

The Oracle's body also serves as a storehouse that is capable of retaining the spirit and information she gleans from each site we visit. Those who were unable to make the trip can draw from the work we did. On many occasions, the beings and energies the Oracle brought through during our travels would speak in subsequent classes back home.

Individual Initiations

Toward the end of every trance, the Master picked ten people to work on individually. For those who had been at the Closing of the Earth's chakras, the Master helped them retrieve the part of themselves they gave to the Earth so many incarnations ago: their courage, their heart, their healing, their knowledge, their joy, their song, and their vision.

The Master would also call attention to the dark and solid aspects that impeded the blending of our bodies and etheric souls. He would have one person take off their shoes, with another he'd press dirt in the face or hair, and with another, he'd have them hold a handful of rocks or a twig he'd plucked off the ground. In this way, he employed the natural elements at hand to emphasize a point. With some, he'd work on their bodies and stretch their necks and backs, all the while naming their shadows.

I will touch each weakness and where you are dark, and allow the dark holes to be filled with light.

Being touched and opened up by the Master heightened the initiatory experience. You never knew what he was going to spotlight, which instilled some dread and trepidation in those who were waiting for their turn. It became our task to stay grounded, to listen and acknowledge what was being touched in us. It might be a point of narcissism, a hoarding level, how we hid from life, or simply that we lacked heart. Lighting up these dark parts proved to be emotionally wrenching for many. While one person was cycling through their indigenous lifetimes, another was conquering a deep-seated fear or working through the pain of their isolation. You can't help reawaken a chakra of the planet without being opened up yourself. Although I couldn't hear everything the Master said to each and every person being touched, what I did hear could have easily applied to me.

When I give you back to yourself, we are also waking up the planet. I will touch that part that will enliven and open you up. Even though the work is with you, it is not with you at all. It is for the planet. You are the key and the doorway.

After being touched by the Master, it felt like a heavy cloak had been lifted from me, which I agreeably shed with elated tears.

Catch the Body

The Teacher's way of leaving at the end of a trance session was always to bless us all and then lift away, allowing the Oracle to ease back into her body. With the more demonstrative Master, it was a mystery as to how he might make his standing exit, or when. There were times he'd toss us a big smooch, "Mwaa!" and blast out. Sometimes, he'd just say, "Catch the body," and we'd scramble to support the Oracle's body as she returned, weary from the enormous amount of energy she'd expended during trance. If we hadn't caught her, she would have collapsed on the spot. In time, we were able to sense when the Master was about to rocket away, and several of us would move into position around her. On a few occasions, the Oracle would come out of trance with her back on top of some willing supporter who was lying on the ground.

The last day in Sedona, we returned to Boynton Canyon and scrambled up a rise off the dirt trail to an open plateau. Rocky cliffs surrounded us on three sides glowing molten gold in the full sun. The Master had us look at the rays of energy streaming in and out of the Oracle's body, waking up the entire mountain range as he restated the importance of abiding by the planetary laws he'd shared with us.

Now, as time goes, on you will learn that these laws have to be incorporated into your lives at some level and that you cannot ignore them quite so easily. At some point you will learn and make gradual changes. Changes that can fit your lifestyle, and into your society in a most appropriate way, and in a balanced way. Don't go home being fanatical. We are not preaching fanatical energy here. Only to a few of you. (!)

Beginnings can be so small as to go unnoticed. Looking back now at our trip to the southwest to open the first chakra of the Earth, I see how it triggered a shift in my sense of self. I went there a human and came back a planetary being. You could say it's just one term of existence exchanged for another, but it's different. A human walks on top of the Earth. A planetary being is the Earth experiencing itself through a sensory body.

The Oracle never predicted how any of us would receive and be impacted by the energy work, nor would the Teacher or the Master. With initiations such as this, it's anyone's guess as to what we would do with our experiences afterwards, given the character of our personalities, our karmic history, and our current lives.

If you are going to move into transformation, you are opening your door to an unknown something, unknown how it is going to touch you, unknown how it is going to impact you. And then you need to bring your choices to it of how you will change.

Back to Balance the First

As one seeks balance they must fight all parts of themselves that don't seek it. For all those parts that have been asleep and numb want to stay that way.

We returned to Sedona and the Grand Canyon the next year to help bring strength and balance to the awakening of the first chakra. We were told that in coming out of its slumber the planet was not any different from a person waking out of a deep sleep — there's an initial boost of brilliant light, blazing with promise and possibility, but then the light diminishes and the reality of the way things are returns.

What you have been seeing in the last year since the awakening has been great negativity on the planet because once there is a great opening there must be a rebalancing, and in rebalancing great negativity can come out. Great droughts, great earthquakes have already hit. Many people have been killed. There have been many problems and they will get worse. You are in a cycle that demands your strength to survive. Not just physically, but emotionally and mentally.

Much like the first trip, the Oracle led the group to each site, listening to a number of sources as she walked, from etheric beings to Earth spirits and ancestral guardians of the land. All of them had something to say and teach, and they pointed her to go here or there so knowledge could be touched and shared. The group might be following her single file along a narrow dirt trail, when she'd come to a dead stop and have us open our "inner ears" to what the land was saying, or she might ask if we felt a sudden shift or wave of energy as we passed through an area. She might suddenly be pulled to go off trail because she was called to a certain place, her body acting like a tuning fork, keying in on the exact location best aligned with the work we had come to do.

"It's my agreement when I go to these places to run that energy," she has shared. "I go there open to those energies coming through as they want to, and when they need to. The force is so strong that it's like being in labor when your body is telling you to push. You have to do it. I step aside a lot, that's my work, so that energy can touch you through my body in a very physical way."

The Oracle never feels controlled or victimized in her heightened state. She has a say in it, a choice to go or not to go where the beings direct her. She's truly at home in her purpose and at her happiest when she is venturing off to new places and connecting with the people and spirits of different lands.

"I'm over-full, constantly receiving and receiving, and letting go and letting go. I get to touch the places and the life forms in their full being. I feel continually nurtured in the connection."

At each site, we repeated a similar routine as with the first trip. We'd circle around the Oracle, who would field questions before bringing in the Master. He would implore us to come into present time, run our energy, and connect with the Earth and each other the best we could without judgment or competition.

Your bodies will be used once again to ride the energy through this planet in this particular spot.

Running energy is amplified when you're joined with like-minded folks who are grounded and connecting back. The more people who are running energy, the more the energy field will be enhanced. Connection requires acceptance and inclusion, like trees in a forest touching each other's roots. It's not just about giving energy; it's also about being open to receiving it, even if you might not like someone or you feel friction with a particular person in the group. We need to transcend personal issues and reach for the higher vibratory rate generated when running energy in unison — we must do it for energy's sake. What's interesting, and almost paradoxical in this dynamic, is how you feel more of who you are. You might be part of a large group, but in this collective emanation your uniqueness is illuminated.

Grounding and moving energy is easier outside on the land. For us, being far away from day-to-day pressures, schedules, and chores gave us an added freedom, which cleared our minds to do the work at hand. Sometimes, in classes, our energy waned over a short period of time. Beings pushed incessantly for us to increase our energy fields, deepen our grounding, and strengthen our connections, but we would stretch and stretch only to flag under the weight of the day. Yet, out here in the floorless, ceiling-less wind and sky of the high desert we could reach without limit — the Earth's energy rising though our feet, feeding our energy fields, and welcoming our willingness to touch it more completely.

As with our previous work in Sedona, the Master would finish each session by selecting ten people to work on one at a time, pointing out areas needing attention and hinting at ways we could bring more balance and strength to our lives. Reaching a state of balance is not a "once and done deal." It requires moment-by-moment rebalancing.

Because you have it one minute doesn't mean you'll have it the next. If you don't know how to laugh with yourself, you'll never have it. Because you're sensitive, you are more prone to mental illness than other people. You are more prone to emotional breakdowns. We're talking about hitting despair so deep that you'll never walk out of it.

So what you will see within yourself is a great deal of darkness come out also, as you have witnessed, all of you have. No one here can't say they haven't. You all have, just as your planet has. You will have to choose your strength to move through them in a healthy way, or you will move into darkness. And the darkness will consume you.

The Cave

Led by a local guide, the last site on our itinerary had us humping up a steep hillside to a cave. The climb was quite difficult for many of us, and we gripped tree branches and bushes to pull ourselves up, some fearfully, some needing a push or a sturdy hand. The stronger helped the less able-bodied, ignoring the guide's words, "Leave the slow ones behind."

Reaching the top of the hill, we gathered in a semicircle at the mouth of a cave.

Not all caves are spiritual caves. Not all caves are alive. This is quite a spiritual cave in that it carries its own life form. The soul has not been damaged, but it has been left alone a long time.

The ancient Indians who were here spoke to the spirit of the cave. You are a bit noisy, a bit rowdy. It does like a bit more respect. I have told it that this is your respect. (!) *But although [we are] noisy, we will leave it clean. The air will be clean. We will not leave debris or harm it in any way possible.*

The Master conveyed once again the struggle we would experience in years to come.

If you believe that the road is an easy road, then you are conning yourself very heavily, and upon yourself you will bring a great deal of grief. It's not wrong to live in a hard way. Much laughter can be brought out of hardness. Much joy can be brought out of hardness. It is learning how to curve like the rock in the cave curves in its hardness that brings balance.

The Master guided us through an exercise in which we were to imagine who we were before we had a name.

Be who you were before you had a name. You can't do it without roots, and you can't do it if your roots are not strong. Be who you were before you had a name, and then let that form fill your body.

At one point, The Master let the cave come in to speak to us. The Oracle's head rotated slowly from side to side as the spirit of the cave scanned the group who stood silent before it. Then, with a gentle, joyful voice, the cave said, "You have brought the Mother[6] to me. I am so happy. Thank you. I have waited for the Mother. You will bring back new life."

---

6. The Mother: A life-bearing and nurturing universal energy that provides structure, a home, and looks to make sure everyone is safe. Mother energy teaches by actions, not just words, and disciplines with caring.

The Pyramids

Egypt

So that in times of darkness, you could look upon us and know that something greater than who you'd become was still inside of you.

The Pyramids

On a drizzly February morning in 1990, we crossed the Giza plateau past camels and Bedouin trinket vendors to the entrance of the Great Pyramid. Seventy-three of us had landed in Egypt to help open the second chakra of the Earth. The second chakra is the seat of life and the center for creation. Although much of the African continent makes up the planet's second chakra, Egypt was the place the chakra had been shut down.

Located between the navel and the pubic bone of the human body, the second chakra is always in creation mode. It provides the fire for physically manifesting all things, from paintbrushes to masterpieces, from construction tools to weapons of war. For a creation to enhance life, however great or small, the second chakra needs to be connected to the fourth, or Heart, chakra. Without the caring of the heart, this fire center can rage out of control, causing chaos and destruction to well-intended creations.

Opening the second chakra of the Earth and in ourselves involved working to blend the dualities of life with death, and good with evil, which had been polarized since humankind became solid.

Every site in Egypt was preselected by *the Librarian,* one of the five beings who make up the Teacher. The Librarian is a humorless, mathematical, master geomancer who can read the energy of places on the planet from topographical maps with exacting detail. The Librarian would pinpoint in advance the areas where we were to work, places chosen for the knowledge still available there, the initiatory energies they radiated, and where the planet's second chakra could best be reawakened. The itinerary was carefully planned out, both from a practical and timely transportation standpoint, and in accord with our capacity to integrate the energies and information as we progressed from one site to the next. Our trance circles no longer required the same standing sentries as were needed in Arizona. In Egypt, there was less concern for Alice (aka evil) coming from outside as from within.

During our travels throughout Egypt, we were asked to perform a number of exercises with an energetic structure of the subtle anatomy oddly named "beast," which we'd been learning about in classes since our trips to Sedona.

Beast

The name "beast"* refers to a physical element of the Earth that exists in the body of every living thing. It's a force every creature on the Earth carries whether it lives on land, in the waters, or in the skies. The word itself raises all kinds of associations, from Godzilla monsters to the demonic, yet it aptly describes a highly physical, Earth-made ingredient we share with all planetary critters, from bees and boa constrictors to bears and buzzards.

The center for beast energy in the human anatomy is located between the first and the second chakras, as well as in the spinal column. The beast, along with the eighth chakra below the feet, helps filter and monitor the amount of Earth energy coming into the human body. From this belly region, the beast energy radiates to the rest of the body.

Wherever you carry a sufficient amount of beast energy in your body is where the planet can "find" your body and share its wisdom and energy with you. People with a good amount of beast energy are fairly grounded. They enjoy living close to nature and growing their own food. They might be involved in groups that are trying to save species from extinction, such as whales, elephants, and old-growth forests. Some have an intuitive knowledge of animals, or the healing properties of plants. Others might have a heightened sense of places, feeling where one area emits a harmful energy, while another is more nurturing.

The Pyramids

Our group lodged first at the Mena House, a traveler's hotel with a rich history of hosting dignitaries from around the world. The hotel's greatest distinction by far is its location, a short walk from the pyramids. Photographs I'd seen didn't prepare me for the escalated feeling of being amidst these colossal limestone and granite structures. I could only imagine how they looked and felt when finished with polished casing stones and caps of solid gold. Their sunlit brilliance must have shone like a lighthouse in interstellar space.

Over the years, exhaustive research has been gathered, speculated, and debated by Egyptologists, archeologists, and astro-archeologists about the origin of the pyramids — who built them and when, how were they constructed, and what was the intent of those who made them? If the accumulated written material on the subject were piled up, it would create a sizable pyramid in itself. What follows is the information related to us from the Teacher and the Master:

The Great Pyramid was built approximately 12,000 years ago. It was not constructed as a tomb for a pharaoh, but as a communication station connected to similar stations on planets in other solar systems. Communicating to kindred beings on other planets through the Great Pyramid required a high level of consciousness. The Pyramid also acted as a power source that generated tremendous electrical energy beyond the field of Earth. However, there's very little energy radiating from it now.

Another, less noticed, aspect of the pyramid complex is the place where it stands. The site chosen to build these mountainous structures was a major energetic hub of the Earth. A "power spot" by today's terminology, only on a mega level. They weren't plugging their generator into a wall socket; they were plugging it into a planetary power plant.

When it was first built, each stone spoke and was completely alive. You would see the vibration of it breathing.

The pyramids' massive blocks of stone, so seamlessly stacked and aligned, were not created by the labor of slaves muscling wooden hoists and levers, but by people remarkably different from us. People whose chakras were larger, more open, and active than ours today. These people had the extrasensory ability of hearing and interacting with stone, just as we would collaborate with another living being. The "living" stones helped them in the construction and told them how they were to be shaped. The pyramid builders were able to move, lift, and set the stones into place sonically, vibrationally, by uttering specific sounds.

The Teacher and the Master told us the pyramids actually stand above an underground city. People didn't enter the Great Pyramid from the outside as we do today. The true entry point to the inside was though granite passages beneath the pyramid.

There are doorways,[7] *but you'd have to know how to open them. Only a certain tone or word would open them. Each door had its name, so you would have to listen to the stone and it would have to give its name.*

Extraordinary strength and knowledge were needed to pass through a succession of chambers and dimensions, seven in all. Those conscious enough to reach the seventh dimension "*...could touch the energy of the Godhead itself.*" Those who did not know how to move through these dimensions might die trying, or come out insane.

As human beings became more solid, the pyramids began to deteriorate. They lost the ability to generate energy and were no longer able to connect to other solar systems. The gold capstone, which utilized the sun's energy like a solar cell, was removed and hidden to prevent anyone from commandeering the pyramid for destructive purposes.

Mention was made of another grouping of pyramids, twenty in number, that are buried now, unseen in the sands of the Saharan desert at a location where the sun's heat is unbearable.

7. Doorways are both physical and etheric portals connecting places on the Earth to the solar system.

Inside the King's Chamber

Musty, acrid smells of dust and urine filled our nostrils as we filed up the long, narrow Grand Gallery. Flanked by mammoth granite blocks, this ascending passageway led us up into the King's Chamber. At the time, gaining entrance to the Great Pyramid was not on an Egyptian tour guide's standard docket. Our travel agent had to arrange it "under the table," with an extra helping of "baksheesh" for a group our size to work in the King's Chamber undisturbed.

We circled in the bare stone room dimly lit by electric light fixtures strung about. The walls were bare and unadorned by any of the paintings, hieroglyphs, or bas-relief typically found in Egyptian tombs. On the floor stood a large, lidless sarcophagus cut from a single block of red granite. The stone had been chipped away, deeply in one corner, seemingly for souvenirs.

There is an empty sarcophagus in this room. It has always been empty. Many people think there used to be a mummy in there, but it has always been empty to symbolize that man should not be buried in a stone structure [and] that all must go back to nature on this planet.

Although the chamber's stone ceilings stood nearly twenty feet high, the space felt close and stuffy, almost airless. The Master had us breathe from our diaphragms in order to find our natural rhythm and sustain it for the duration of the session. He told us we were there to shut down the pyramid's operational level of the stone, which would allow the edifice to go back to nature.

Let nature take back what belongs to nature so it may move into the law of development. It will take approximately forty years for its demise — when the stone will no longer be living and the crumbling will occur even more. Probably not in your lifetime, [but] in Nature's time. So you won't see these stones collapsing when you walk out. (!)

Working to Separate Beast from Soul

As stated earlier, the beast is an Earth energy source embodied in all planetary life forms, from gnats to whales. As human beings became solid, the domination of the natural world began. This solidity not only enslaved the beast, it also held part of the etheric soul imprisoned, locked in the physical body, unable to return home to the oversoul.[8] It was a dysfunctional relationship if ever there was one.

The way home is to let go of the beast. You are visitors. This has never been your home. The beast must have its home, too. Acknowledge that you are sharing this home with the beast — meaning this planet. This is its home. You must allow the home to be what it is and not destroy it. Not have it all your way, which is what souls have been doing for a long time.

It is time to decide with the heart if you are going to allow the beast to be separate. You can truly not connect to anything until you can separate from it.

By separating the beast from our soul, we are better able to see who we are as an etheric soul, and who we are as a body. When you're merged with another life form, you lose self-awareness of who you are as a being. Our work was to first detach the beast and soul, then begin to reconnect them in a healthy way that is not merged, possessive, or domineering, but mutually beneficial to both.

Although we'd done some preliminary work in classes, the real separation of beast and soul began in the King's Chamber of the Great Pyramid. This was not an easy task. Even with a

8. Oversoul: A person's etheric soul is a particle of its oversoul, or great soul. The life experiences and knowledge we gain in the physical world are shared with the oversoul. Much like how a river unites with the ocean, when the body dies the etheric soul joins with its ocean, the oversoul, and the education of that particular lifetime joins a larger source.

great deal of assistance from spiritual guides, this was by no means a simple release. They had been closely enmeshed in us for lifetimes, and separation required concentrated attention and ongoing energetic exercises well beyond the duration of this trip.

Tibetan monks take years and lifetimes to learn how to separate beast from soul, so don't be ashamed if you're having trouble with it.

We were asked to run energy and move our etheric souls to the top of the pyramid, while our beast was to remain touching the stone. The Master toned to call the beast out, and for the sound of the beast and the stone to connect.

Let Nature for this moment be the supreme deity to this planet. For a moment, know the true parent of who you are, that which has given your body life, this Earth. Nature is the parent. It is the second chakra that brings life.

The Master informed us that the spirit of the pyramid, which was still alive in the stones, wanted to come in and touch each one of us in order to say goodbye and to reclaim its life.

THE GREAT PYRAMID

There once was a time when this land was very fertile and very green and very beautiful. We came from very far away and we built these structures to house us and to bring us back to where we could find all our beloved that we lost. We cut the stone because it was a living stone and it could house all the memories of who we were in its life. Now stand among the stones, let it speak to you. Its memory is your memory. Its life is your life.

In this chamber of no light. In this chamber of no sky, no moon, no sun, remember your home. Go back to your home. Touch the stone if you need to. Do not touch the loss but the joy. Receive the joy. Receive your name.

We were asked to step up to the Oracle one at a time and state our names. In response, the Great Pyramid gave each of us our ancient names, thanked us, and said goodbye. The ancient names we were given were the names of our souls, which we had orally embedded into the stones of the pyramid when it was built. Now it was returning these names to us. The names were of a different language, yet a few sounded surprisingly similar to names people had been given this lifetime. To some, the pyramid shared a past life. A few were told they'd participated in the architecture of its construction.

Later, the Teacher informed us that he didn't know in advance how the Great Pyramid would receive us, or if it would even speak to us and give us our ancient names.

It has basically learned not to trust bodies. You can understand why with all the destruction inside. But it was most pleased and actually came in and spoke. It means that your energy was acceptable. And that you were in a non-destructive mode — at least for the moment. (!)

At the time, we didn't know our ancient names would serve as a vocal key in our forthcoming guided imagery work.

Saqqara

The site chosen next took us south of Cairo to the step pyramid in Saqqara, which predated the pyramids of Giza. Although eroded by time, I felt warmth in my heart standing beside it, like reuniting with a dear old friend.

We were asked to remember being in the catacombs beneath the step pyramid, and to recall how the area looked when it was lush with vegetation — a time when the pyramid's angular steps were filled in, giving it a fluid, waveform profile.

Step Pyramid at Saqqara

All this sand was not here. This was not a great desert then. But you foresaw it would become a great desert. Now remember in this day consciousness and life were one and the same. This is before the great possession of the beast.

Say your ancient names and walk down the street. Feel the life. Feel the sadness that you knew things were coming to an end. And let the beast feel the grief for what is now.

The Master had us form a circle with our arms linked to one another. He asked us to say aloud, "I am here," followed by our ancient names. After everyone in the circle had spoken his or her name, the Master described a ceremony we'd undertaken inside the step pyramid ages ago. In that ceremony, we had also linked arms, spoken our names, and then dropped our arms and said goodbye to each other — because we knew what was about to transpire — how we would become solid, and there was nothing we could do to stop it.

You knew you would become enemies to each other. Such as you loved each other, you would know hate for each other. And such as you cared for each other, you would only know pain. And since the body was going to be enslaved, you knew you'd make each other slaves.

I scanned the faces in the circle around me in present time as the story resounded a tone of sorrow deep inside me.

You will not drop your arms now, as you [did when you] formally said your goodbyes. Formally say your hellos to each together now in your ancient names. Do so with the heart and the second chakra together. It means touching each other and not ignoring all the history, but forgiving the history.

The Master then toned.

True toning emits specific vibrations that help open hearts and chakras. It's similar to how the stomata of leaves respond to bird song, or how listening to your favorite music touches more completely who you are. The soul responds to sound, just as the body does. In our work, the toning would also help us bond together as a group. Sometimes it would be melodic, other times it would soar to piercing heights or dive deep to cavernous levels. This is interesting, because the Oracle's personal vocal range cannot reach the highs and lows the Master and other beings express through her body. In fact, the Oracle herself is tone deaf.

SAQQARA PYRAMID

You came back.

Do you still hate? There is no truth in hate. There is no truth in revenge. Are you here to help me die so that I may live more? You cannot hate and help me die. You don't have to love more. Just don't hate.

I feel the heart. This is good. But the life seat is so damaged. I am sorry for you. You will need a great deal of caring to bring health back to the life seat. As long as the life seat is damaged you will not know how to bring life without hate.

Feel the heart and the seat of life together. Feel the stone in both, and let the stone's energy and life come into both. Give me the beast. I give you back your sky.

Pineal Movies

Something startling happened that night in my Mena House hotel room. While lying in bed attempting to sleep, my attention was drawn to pressure in the center of my forehead above the bridge of my eyebrows.

My third eye had turned ON.

This was something I'd never experienced before. It felt like a switch had suddenly been thrown, and at the foot of the bed a procession of moving pictures flickered in the air. At first, I discounted it as an illusion, a borderline dream state. Closing my eyes did not affect the steady stream of images in any way. Much like a projector in a movie theatre, a cone of light shone from a tiny aperture in my brain. Annoyed at first, I sought to calm it down. But there was no stopping it. So I surrendered and settled into viewing the spectre of pictures rapidly shuttling before my eyes. It took awhile to adjust the speed of my perception to match the frequency of the pictures being shown. In time, I realized these were not dream-like visions but images of actual experienced events — not in my recent past, but far back in time.

How was this happening, and why? I had never had such experiences before. Was it the energy work we were doing? Given the circumstances, I could only assume that something had been triggered while staying in such close proximity to the pyramids. Being such a powerful engine of energy, perhaps they had awakened a highlight reel of past-life memories, which were then projected through the "magic lantern" of my third eye.

My wife and a couple other fellow travellers had similar experiences. We've since referred to this episode as "pineal movies." None of the places we've visited since have produced similar effects. I wish I'd had a bedside notebook and written down the many sights I was shown those two nights at the Mena House before time evaporated them like dew to the dawn.

The Sphinx

The following morning was cold. We gathered around the Oracle near the base of the Sphinx. Tiers of wooden scaffolding had been erected in front of the face of the monument for its restoration. Standing in the limestone shadow of the huge lion's body with the head of a human strangely coincided with our work with the beast and the soul.

We were told the Sphinx was built around the same time as the Great Pyramid, and that the subterranean chambers constructed deep beneath it were even older.

They put a monument on top of a very sacred temple. They felt that if they built this monument above it nothing would inhibit the temple below. It will not be found in your lifetime. But it will be found shortly, especially as people are more able to use the information in more correct ways.

The Master again clarified the work we were attempting to do in separating the beast from our soul, and how we needed to reconnect to the beast and the Earth in a respectful, interdependent way.

You have to learn to work with the beast, since you are alive with the beast. That's the good news. I see this has thrilled you completely. (!)

We were asked to run our energy and repeat our ancient names as we visualized descending into the chambers below the Sphinx to connect with the beings residing there — who, we were told, were old friends of ours from long ago.

Connection comes from the heart and the seat of life. It does not come from your comfort zone. If you wait until only you are comfortable you will never connect.

The Master brought in one of the non-physical beings who live within the chambers below the Sphinx. This being was surprised at how short our bodies had become. In their time, human beings stood ten feet tall. The being guided us through a series of visualizations into the underground chambers below the Sphinx to further help us separate and then reconnect our beast with our souls. As our etheric souls and physical bodies become united in a more cooperative way we will not be able to conceal it from the outside world or keep it mute. On the contrary, we'll be living it, and our presence will highlight the karma in others.

The being who lives in the chamber below the Sphinx told us his name, *ANAK*, and spoke to us, saying:

All that you touch this day forward will know their karma to the beast. You will not be well-loved. You will be despised, and you will never be able to hide this information anymore. Those who love to possess and destroy hate the truth.

Do not die with it. Stay alive with it and come back home. And do no more destruction with it, or it will destroy you. You, meaning the ancient one, not you that stands before me that is such a stranger.

The people in our group experienced the guided visualizations and energy work in different ways. Some saw vivid pictures or colors; others felt it as a body sensation or experienced an inner knowing. Even with guidance, I was not adept at seeing the visuals presented to us, such as those in the chambers we were taken through under the Sphinx. Although the others might have perceived or sensed the subterranean surroundings immediately, envisioning was more of a time-release process for me — as my perception expanded the more open-bodied and energy-conscious I became.

The beast and soul work continued as the group traveled on to Aswan, where we boarded the Melodie, a chartered boat that took us up the Nile River with stops along the way. The Master gave us a nod of compassion in our efforts to detach the unhealthy and long standing relationship between our beast and our etheric souls.

I understand it is very hard to remove the beast, or to feel the separation between beast and soul. You've been this way for thousands of years. I'm not expecting you to do it perfectly in the next week or two.

Bringing Life and Death Together

Life has death and death has life.

With the solidification of human beings ages ago, the life-death cycle was severed. No longer was death perceived as a natural transition to another living state that fed and fertilized life. It was deemed the end. A void of nothing. The continuum was broken, and along with it good and evil became polarized.

In order for your fourth and second chakras to be in harmony, you must have life and death on a simultaneous level, and you must be able to bring good and evil together as one.

Ancient Egypt presents a vivid example of the separation of life and death. This is where bodies were intentionally mummified, their organs removed and sealed in jars. Rather than letting the body return to the Earth, its maker, through natural decomposition, people exerted significant time and effort in deliberately seeking to suspend its decay — for the purpose of ensuring a plentiful afterlife.

The Oracle pointed out, "When we made death a bad thing, a fearful thing, it separated us from nature's life-death cycle.* When we began to kill for joy, revenge, or to be dominant, we created a disconnection with the Supreme Being. Murder disengages life from death. It breaks the continuum and puts a crack in life."

The cycle of life and death occurs simultaneously. Whatever dies naturally contributes to the life cycle, much like a fallen old growth tree fertilizes and passes on living information to the young trees. So, even in death there is sound and connection that allows life to flourish. Only through this life-death cycle can consciousness continue becoming. They are, in essence, one and the same. Yet when the continuous creative interplay of life and death is severed we lose a great deal of the wisdom and experience we gained in our lifetime. As one Earth Being put it, "You take all the losses with you and come back in the next lifetime lesser than what you were."

For the Oracle, the blending of Life and Death gives her a feeling of completeness. "I am at home and very present. There's no past or future, only the here and now."

In working to embody the blending of life and death, we were introduced to a triangular energy system in our spiritual anatomy, which needed development.

The Triangular System

The triangular system is a geometric structure that exists in each person's energy body at a deeper level than the chakras. Everyone is born with this structure inside his or her body. It consists of three separate triangles:

One triangle starts at the eighth chakra and points up to the third chakra. One comes from the ninth chakra and points down to the fifth chakra. The third, middle triangle, points from the third to the fifth chakra.

According to the Teacher: *The universe runs on circular patterns, but the triangular system carries the biggest impact of energy.*

The purpose of the triangular system is to expand the body's capacity to contain more energy. This structure, which later became three-dimensional pyramids, is one of the strongest living forms. It allows us to bring in more fiery Earth energy without harming the body.

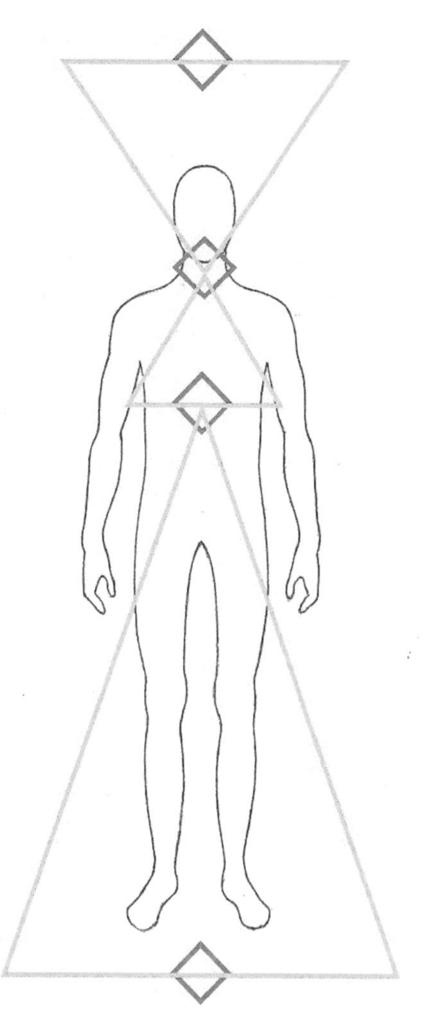

The Master shared how the pyramids were consciously designed in the shape of the triangular system embodied in the bodies of their creators. In order for us to feel the triangular system in our bodies, we needed our etheric souls and bodies to touch and blend. He told us that if we had the right amount of energy in our third chakras, and all our chakras were open and complete, we would be able to move immense stones, such as those erected for the pyramids.

Death in the Desert

Do not make Death your enemy.

The Master sought out a remote place for us to meet Death. The site needed to be out in the desert away from the hubbub of humanity. Our tour guides must have thought we were out of our minds when it was determined we needed to land our chartered boat on the west bank of the river, far from ancient ruins, museums, or tourist shops, with only the vastness of unending sand spreading west to the horizon into the Sahara. Ramps were extended on the shore for us to disembark. We gathered in the sand around the Oracle as she brought in the Master.

We are in a very desolate area. This is not your domain. This is the beast's domain.

You now have an element of death all around you, although life is being sustained here at all times and in all places. I am going to bring in the energy of Death. I would suggest you find where you are alive.

Give Death your ancient name, and do this from the seat of life and from your heart. It will say a few words to you. The impact should be enormous. It will not be light. It will not be joyful. It will be Death.

It was not the most pleasant of preambles. Yet, this was not the spooky, skull-faced, grim-reaper Death that is represented in graveyard stories and horror movies, but true Death brimming with vibrant activity.

DEATH

Death is not a place that is lonely, and it is not a place of isolation or solitude. It is a place of many voices and of many things. Life intermingles with Death and brings the heart to it. Great caring and great loving are in Death as much as in Life. All that you are, you bring to me in death, and I, in death, will give you back to life as you are, who you are, all that you are.

I will give you a gift. When l touch you with your deaths and you bring forth your life, if your life is agony, give me your agony. If your life is desperation, give me your desperation. If it is joy, give me that. Give me all and I will give you complete death. Then you will understand much better. But, if you hold back, I will add to your agony. I will add to your pain. Give me all that you can and I will match you, or I will not. Do you understand?

One at a time, we stepped up to the Oracle to be touched by Death as we worked to radiate the combined energies of our second chakra and heart chakra. When one person showed fear, Death asked for courage. When another held back their life, Death urged them to reach for it, or find their heart and give of it freely.

Later, the Master had the following words to share about our meeting with Death.

If Death touched you in a place that was not known it would be quite fearful and quite exhausting to your bodies.

There is not one person here who is free of evil. There is not one person here who is free of blame, shame, or guilt. There is not one person here who is so clear as to call himself perfect. So when a few get a piece of their dark side and others feel wonderful, possibly a little compassion would be helpful to those who receive hard information because your turn is next.

We continued to work on blending the polarities of life and death as we journeyed up the Nile, stopping at old ruins where Death would speak to us again.

DEATH

Now find your correct death mode. Find a way in which you may die in this body so that you may acquire the release, the letting go truly that is death. Not how you are going to die in this particular body — your death mode. This is the key to not just die, but to live in your death.

Do not block me, but blend with me.

You will see good and evil together. It is my companion. Death/life, good/evil we are companions. If these were together would your world be so hard? If you walk with death and you give life to death continually, you will carry the law of death so that evil would have to blend with good and do you no more harm.

Traveling further north, we stopped at Luxor, Karnak, and the Valley of the Kings. Everywhere we went, the Oracle's body served as a battery helping to open the second chakra of the Earth. The energy work and travel from site to site made for long, hard days, extending well beyond nightfall. This was purposefully initiatory, stretching our endurance, wearing down our controls, and testing us to see how we would operate in a more formless state.

Initiations are experiences that touch every part of us that is solid and fearful. They bring out the voice inside that says we can't make it — the voice that stops us from growing into more of who we are. They challenge all the learning we've gained with real situations in the here and now. When we don't get our way and our comforts are removed, will we still connect? Do we care for one another? Do we allow others to be who they are? Can we let go of our expectations in order to touch our strengths? Do we ask for help, and will we have the willingness to receive it in the way it comes?

From Cairo we bussed to Sinai, the long wedge of land situated between the Red Sea and the Gulf of Aqaba. Part way down the coastline we stopped at a beach. It was just what our dry bodies needed. Many of us dug our bare feet in the wet sand along the windy shore to feel the cool, tidal water of the Red Sea ride up our ankles, which we were told was the holiest of waters.

WATERS OF THE RED SEA

All great prophets have come to this part, and must come to join the life of the water as you are doing. Only water can touch the soul. Not even the wind can speak to the soul. The wind belongs to the Earth. So does fire. Only water touches the spirit and can give life and connection of spirit and body. Water is the embodiment of the soul. Why were the pyramids built so close to me? Because I was the soul's life. I am the embodiment of the soul's life.

The Red Sea was asked if it would share the biblical story of Moses parting its waters as he led the Israelites across what was then known as the Sea of Reeds.

WATERS OF THE RED SEA

You wish the truth? (Yes.)

They came across forty meters down, but at that time it was much less water, and they moved across the water, and in so moving across the water they created more path than what was there. They created trenches along the way. Water filled the trenches and soldiers coming to them became stuck in the trenches. And slowly they sunk. The soldiers did not all die. Many returned home, but let the Israelites go freely onto their way. The waters did not part.

The Waters of the Red Sea had us go back millions of years to touch the continuum of what once was, what the sea was like at that time.

As you achieve life and death, as you bring together good and evil, as these two forms come back together, feel my continuum in you.

You do this well. You have been well trained. Touch my strength. You will need my strength in this life to come and others to come.

Mt. Sinai

Those places that were most holy were put in places that were difficult to get to because they're not supposed to be lived in. Sedona is not supposed to be lived in. Mt. Sinai is not supposed to be lived on or in.

We arrived in the dark, the night clear and stellar. Looming over us, a range of mountains rose in silhouette above the desert floor. Our lodging consisted of a cluster of stone, single-story guest cottages linked by pathways. It looked pleasant enough, but something about the place felt off kilter to me. At 3:00 a.m., I awoke with intense abdominal cramps. By dawn, I was nauseous, drained by diarrhea, and feeling the first waves of frustration sinking in. We'd be bussing back to Cairo the following day and I didn't want to miss this chance to climb one of the most sacred mountains of the world.

Despite how awful I felt, I managed to get to the buses in the morning to see everyone off. I sat on a rock, pale and wobbly, unwilling to give up. I boarded the bus, which then dropped us off near the famous seventh century monastery of St. Catherine. I could barely walk. While the group was touring the monastery, taking in its archive of Byzantine art, religious relics, and house of skulls, I was puking over the monastery's ancient rock wall. The vomiting cleared the nausea for a spell. I lumbered on in slow motion. As my wife and I entered the courtyard of the monastery, we were informed there was a camel around the corner waiting to carry me halfway up the mountain.

The Sinai Range

The camel's name was "Samson." His master, "Ahmed," a short Bedouin man with leather-like skin baked by the Sinai sun and wind, walked alongside my wife. Samson's slow loping stride and tramp of hooves on the rocky path made me more woozy. It took everything I had to hang on, gripping the hard knob of the saddle like a lifeline. I could see the path's switchbacks unfold ahead like a ribbon speckled with hikers inching along in slow motion up the barren, granite mountainside. Gaining altitude, I recalled what our guide had said about the importance of one's mental state while climbing Mt. Sinai. "Best not do too much talking or thinking. Keep your thoughts on the path and your mind focused."

The 7,500-foot mountain is not high by mountaineering standards, but the challenge comes in ascending its seven levels, which can exert something different on each person's body and psyche, and require extra energy to go beyond. One fellow traveler pointed out how it was a struggle for her to walk. "Looking back, I believe it was because of my disconnection with the Earth," she said.

It will be hard for some people to climb, not because the climb is particularly hard, although it is, but because of moving through the time levels.

Approaching a Bedouin tent at one turn. I demanded to get off Samson. I was reeling. I lay my body out on the hard ground. I could go no further. Ragged tent fabric flapped in the wind above my head. My wife explained to Ahmed how sick I was. He answered her in Arabic. She was able to decipher the Arabic word for tea, and he had one of the Bedouins at the tent heat up a cup of "habat," an herb tea they drink for upset stomach.

The tea was dark and hot. It tasted like sage. Within ten minutes after drinking it, I was ready to keep going. Samson took me as far as camels could go. From there the path narrowed and curved up a rocky gorge to where 750 steep, stone steps began. A brisk wind pushed at our backs, urging us on. Surprisingly, the higher I ascended the better I felt.

It wasn't an easy hike for the Oracle either, huffing and puffing, all the time wondering where the life force of the mountain was. "It felt like every doorway was closed, she said. "There wasn't any sound coming through. They were all locked." It was not until she stood on the summit and could see the entire range of honey-colored mountains that the spirit of the area came alive.

"All the doors opened like a book. It's not just one spiritual mountain. It's like a forest, only of mountains instead of trees, and each mountain has something to give."

We circled around her, breathing in the sunny, rarefied air as she brought in the Master.

When the laws were given on this mountain to Moses and brought down to the people, it was to unite them into one level. It is not that you have to just not kill, "Thou shalt not kill." But "thou" will not think about killing another. That your energy is as important as the action. The thought is as strong as the actual action.

That's what these laws were trying to speak about. Many of you in your solidity believe that as long as you don't do it, you're okay. Much of the world believes this. It's not that somebody is going to come down and punish you. It's not that the sun is going to move closer to the planet and burn you up. But the thought at some point has to meet a creation or an action.

The Master brought in a life essence to energize the triangular system in our bodies and connect us to the ocean of life.

As I stood in the circle working to open up to the Sinai energy, I saw how my frail climbing experience had instilled a new, guiding principle: when you commit to your path, obstacles are bound to threaten and tempt you to surrender. Help might not be readily at hand, but with perseverance, an open mind, and no expectations assistance will come in surprising ways and from unknown places — in the form of a camel hidden around a corner, a cup of tea brewed in a Bedouin tent, or a boost from an updraft of mountain air. At the tour's farewell banquet in Cairo, our Egyptian guides honored me for being, "The first corpse to ever climb Mt. Sinai."

Busting Old Beliefs

Before leaving Egypt for home, the Teacher had some insightful thoughts for us to ponder.

When we talk about becoming a more conscious human being we're talking about an adventure of a lifetime. For many of you who entered this work, you came in thinking you would be better than anyone else, that nothing bad would ever happen to you, that it would make you wonderful, special, or more abundant, to get anything you want, to visualize and therefore it is. So obviously when a problem hit and visualization didn't help, then everything was wrong, outside of you and inside of you.

Look at your belief systems of what this work is supposed to be. What did you want this work to give you? What did it mean to become more conscious? This is not supposed to hurt you; this is simply to start touching belief systems in your self that are sacred.

So, if Mt. Sinai is a cathedral of the world, that cathedral symbolizes spiritual and/or conscious work. It symbolizes what it is to come to the body, and for the body to come to the soul.

It took tremendous strength and will; it took courage and it took lots of help and connectedness to climb the mountain. And it took faith that if you couldn't make it, you would have help.

Now allow the truth of one of the most sacred places on the planet to question your belief system, or break it up, if you will. To live there what would it require? You would need to find water. You'd need the support of the area to help you, wouldn't you? You would need tools to live there. So that which is sacred is not easy is it? That which is sacred and holy is not given freely.

Oh, I do like breaking these belief systems.

Mt. Roraima

Venezuela

The third chakra is the home of karma.

Crossing a rocky streambed en route to the village of Paraitepui, the trailer, which was hitched to the Toyota four-wheeler, became entrenched. As our guides assessed how to free the trailer without having to unload all the backpacks and supplies, we strolled around, taking in the scenery. The bites on our arms and legs had already begun to itch and welt where sand flies had feasted on us the previous night camping off the road in the Grand Savannah.

The area around Paraitepui was once a rainforest. Spindly trees, blackened by flame, stood as skeletal remnants of the fire that had burned the area some years before. Highways of ants trucked blades of grass to four-foot tall mounds built of excavated dirt. In the distance, the *tepuis* (mountains) of Roraima and Kukenan towered above the land. Their vertical walls and table-top summits resembled the mesas in the American southwest that rise like fortresses of stone straight out of the desert floor. But the similarity ends there. These are weather-makers, rain cloud magnets, with waterfalls streaming down their flanks.

I watched a veil of rain pass across the sheer escarpment of Roraima, the crystal mountain we had come to climb. It was the end of June 1991. We'd flown to Venezuela to help open the third chakra of the planet and to reawaken it in ourselves. We had no idea what lay before us, only that we'd been duly forewarned. The Teacher had made it clear that the third chakra would be the hardest, most difficult of our travels. He was right.

When you became completely solid you killed the third chakra. So, this is not supposed to be easy, because you are attempting to bring it back to life.

In the human body the third chakra is located in the solar plexus area of the abdomen. The function of this energy center is to integrate etheric energy with physical energy. It is a junction center where the fluid timing of our souls is to blend with the physical timing of our bodies. As we became more solid, this exchange became disrupted and the flow stopped; we lost consciousness of the timing of our bodies, and of nature. Our lives became more selfish, materialistic, and for countless lifetimes we treated the planet like a slave, a resource for the taking. Now, attempting to open our third chakras would mean having to face the karma of our arrogance, our self-entitlement, and the pain of our destructive acts.

The third chakra is a highly unconscious place in all of you because that's the place you dramatically stopped. You stopped the flow, you stopped the level of integration, you stopped the Kundalini.

Kundalini

The Kundalini is a fiery energy of the Earth that flows through the meridians of the planet. This energy is governed by the beast, and when correctly awakened in a human body it can expand consciousness by helping to bring more etheric energy into the body from the Earth in a way the body can absorb it.

The kundalini is a very strong belief system in eastern religion. It's not a chakra point, but certainly a point in the body that once opened puts the body in a different energy band, so your body can become more conscious.

Caution should be noted. Kundalini energy will highlight areas in the body that are solid or fixed. If the heart and other energy centers of the body are not open, the fierce fire of the kundalini can overcome the body, causing all manner of torment and pain. A spiritual emergency or identity crisis might result when a person's perception or personal sense of reality, values, or beliefs undergo such a seismic shift. What can be misdiagnosed as schizophrenia, or psychosis, might be a spontaneous transformational process triggered by the entry or amplification of kundalini in the body.

The kundalini brings light to the shadows. Not only is it bringing light to the shadows it's bringing them up. Kundalini work is very dangerous work. It's only truly ever been successfully done by monks or [other] people who have devoted their entire life to this work. But when a planet upgrades its level, it brings up kundalini to everything and everyone. Every living thing. So, it doesn't matter if you're a monk or what you've devoted your life to.*

Due to the supervision we were given by the Teacher, no one in our group experienced the amount of distress that can come when the kundalini is awakened in the body unregulated. It took years of running our energy before the Teacher felt we had the structures in place and the capability of inviting this fiery energy into our bodies. The pyramid system introduced to us in Egypt assisted us in safely raising our level of Kundalini without our bodies becoming overwhelmed by it.

The Oracle shared how the kundalini changed her life. When she was eighteen years old, she signed up to join the U.S. Air Force because she felt it would help her obtain a college degree. Her plans were dramatically interrupted by a kundalini episode that blew open the doors of her trance mediumship. Ironically, she'd grown up believing that psychic stuff and fortune telling was nonsense. Then it exploded in her. She felt lost, unstable, and a bit crazy until she found help and psychic guidance. "The kundalini burns whatever is in the way," she said. "It might be one of the hardest growth times in your life, because you have to choose your strength in your weakest moment. It's like the Phoenix, the bird that burns to ash, only to rise again with a new life, a new path."

Opening the Third Chakra

In order for it [the third chakra] to open up, in order for it to become a functioning chakra, it has to integrate with the soul. It has to come to terms with an integration process within the soul and the body. When the connection was broken is when the soul said, "I will not be connected with the Earth." It possessed the Earth. "Everything on this Earth belongs to me."

The purpose is to bring the [soul and body] together. Now, this has never been attained on this planet by souls with bodies. Does this give you the scope of how difficult this is?

Mt. Roraima

The 9,000-foot mountain is located on the borders of Venezuela, Brazil, and Guyana. The region, it is said, inspired Sir Arthur Conan Doyle's book, *The Lost World.* Roraima is one of 144 tepuis in the area that are considered some of the oldest geological formations on Earth, dating back two billion years. All together, the tepui system represents the beginning of time on the Earth, when the continents of Africa and South America were one.

All mountain ranges come and go. Lakes come and go. Oceans change. All land masses change. The tepuis will never be gone — they are in all dimensions of this planet. You can go to the very beginning of the planet and the very end, and you will see that whole tepui range. Nowhere else can you say that on this planet.

More than sixty students of the Teacher signed up for the Venezuelan trip, which would include traveling to Canaima, Angel Falls, and the Orinoco River. Unfortunately, the first leg of climbing Mt. Roraima had to be limited to twenty-six, which was the maximum number of people the Venezuelan tour company agreed to guide up the mountain. So the Master selected those students who had the most karma to reclaim on Roriama.

The plan had been for us to start hiking to the mountain the day we arrived at the Paratepui village, but the porters were late so we had to wait a day. No one seemed annoyed by the delay. Releasing expectations and surrendering control had become familiar companions on these trips. Some folks used the time to re-organize their packs and to see what carrying forty-plus pounds on their backs felt like. Later in the day, we circled around the Oracle. Our Venezuelan guides were invited to join the circle and meet the Master.

It's a wonderful place you are going to with many life forms. But more than that it is the life of the core of the planet itself, and in that sense you will begin to feel more of the Earth's energy and spirit energy in a connecting way. Roraima brings up the core because it is a huge crystal. So it brings up the whole timing piece by itself.

The Master asked us to run our energy, to open our third chakras, allow the beast to help us ground to the Earth, invite the kundalini, and to connect our etheric souls with our genetic entity.

The Genetic Entity

The *genetic entity* is a living etheric form located in the upper neck and throat area of the human anatomy. It is called the genetic entity because it is part of the DNA structure of the body. It works to connect the energy and information of the etheric soul, which comes in through the seventh chakra, with the physical body. It is through the genetic entity that the etheric soul is able to touch our heart.

Although science has yet to invent a lens that can detect the genetic entity or see the chakras of the human anatomy, for that matter, it appears psychically as nerve clusters in the shape of a three-pronged fork or trident. One prong resonates to the upper chakras, one resonates to the lower chakras, and the center prong reaches down to the back of the heart where it resonates with the middle chakras.

The stronger the genetic entity, the stronger the consciousness of the body. The more you are connected and working with your body, the more the genetic entity evolves. A healthy genetic entity has a lot of colors, combining all the earth tones of a healthy physical body with the brilliant pastel colors of the soul.

As we ran our energy, the Master brought in the tone of the mountain for us to attune our bodies to its energy frequency in a way that would help us during our ascent.

Later in the day, we sat on the floor of a mud brick building that served as the schoolhouse for the village. Above our heads, incessant rain battered the thatch roof. Roraima was saying hello with a tumultuous demonstration of its intensity. The rain hammered the ground with such ferocity it felt like it was trying to drive its riot of water all the way through the planet and out the other side.

We left the Paraitepui village the next morning on foot. The two-day, twenty-five mile trek to the base camp at the bottom of Roraima was taking a toll on the Oracle. At the time, her body was quite large; built like a buffalo with "short, Polish, peasant legs" — in her words. In no time, her ankles began to swell, and with it, her irritation. She didn't like camping. She was dirty. There wasn't enough food, and the food we were given was not that good. Also, the amount of energy she was exerting through her third chakra was draining her and straining the third chakras of the men who walked alongside at her slow, stop and go pace. "It was intense," as one of them put it. "Like walking next to an energy vortex."

While camping that rainy night along the Kukenan River, it was decided the men would alternate walking with the Oracle in two hour shifts the next day, and also that the group would not get too strung out along the path. On every trip, the Oracle works to sustain an energetic connection with the entire group, day and night. Rays of energy spread from her body to each one of us, creating a more unified field. These rays can become stretched beyond her endurance if people roam too far away or detach themselves from the group. It's our job to keep this connection intact and strong. If we drift or disconnect, a link is broken and a gap is created, which can weaken the amount of energy needed to do the work. The Oracle's energy field has to then fill the void, demanding even more from her.

I recall stopping at one point along the trail to allow her a "whine break." She shared how she hated doing the hike, wanted to take a shower, put on clean clothes, and go shopping. Around us a steady breeze sifted through blades of savannah grass. Looking up at the mountain I could see sections of "la rampa," the diagonal green path we'd be climbing to a notch near the top, and I wondered how, given the Oracle's physical discomfort and lack of conditioning, she was ever going to hoof it up there.

The others had reached base camp before we did and had set up their tents. I explored the area with my tent mate. We followed a narrow rivulet to a large boulder bejeweled with orchids, pitcher plants, mosses, lichens, and tiny flowers, whose names I didn't know. We circled the rock in awe, filling our eyes with shapes and colors until our attention was drawn to two Pemon Indian porters thirty feet away who were hopping up and down as they fired rocks with slingshots at two venomous snakes.

In the morning, the porters went ahead of the group hauling tents and supplies in woven baskets on their backs aided by straps stretched taut across their foreheads. We were each given a sandwich bag with a stick of dried mystery meat, a knuckle of cheese, a few raisins, and a little chunk of chocolate. This would be our food for the duration of the ascent. We learned later the reason for the meager rations was because the tour guides believed our group of mostly middle-aged Americans would run out of gas, stop midway up the mountain, and turn back.

In the beginning, the trail was a muddy mush that sliced through an emerald garden of moss-cloaked limbs, tree ferns and carnivorous plants, some of which were large yellow-green veined vases, while others were quite minute, growing right out of rock. Everywhere a chorus of dripping water filled our ears. Higher up the vegetation thinned, opening up to cliffs and an ever-changing sky with passing clouds and showers. For the Oracle, the climb was like trudging through sludge. The higher we hiked the more her body strained, and for good reason — as we later found out — in a lifetime long ago she'd been murdered on Roraima.

The medium's body was going through its death over and over again.

As it turns out, the Oracle wasn't the only one who'd died on the mountain in a past life. Climbing onto a stony precipice, I entered a mist that drifted off a high waterfall. The whisper-soft droplets tapping my face detonated a bomb of grief and loss in my heart, and I immediately broke into heaving, uncontrollable sobs for no apparent reason.

Every single person had a window at that waterfall — very large windows.[9] *Please understand that we did have it set up for you not to die. If anyone was there to push you through, you could have died. Or if you chose to go.*

Higher still, we clambered up a slope of loose scree, taking two steps forward and one step back. When asked, "How much further to the top?" the recurring answer from the guides was, "Not far. Fifteen minutes." They didn't know about the Oracle's steel-trap mind, and how she locks onto the information she receives. Then when it doesn't happen the way she's been told, it hits her body like a lie. So, when another fifteen minutes had passed, and another, with still a long way to go to reach the sum-

9. Windows: These are preset times, initiated by one's causal self,* when the soul is to be born into a physical body, as well as the times when the body will die. We are given a number of birth and dying windows, and we do not live beyond the last window.

mit, the Oracle's body reacted as if she'd been betrayed. Whether the guides were saying it to encourage us, or they were not noting the pace of our progress, it only made the trying situation worse and the Oracle's agitation more intense.

Darkness was setting in as those assisting the Oracle finally made it to the top of the mountain. But to reach the camp we still had to thread and scramble through a black maze of rock in a light, steady rain. The Oracle lumbered along looking grim; her body racked with pain and utterly spent of energy. "I'm not going to make it," she said.

We were working to keep you alive. We knew the medium's body would have a very hard time getting up and down. She died on Roraima. She has been killed there. The men who helped her were sacrificed there also.

Flashlight beams probed for passages through the puzzle of wet stone as night filled in the shadows around us. We finally made it, hefting, pushing, and pulling the Oracle out of the maze to an open area where tents had been set up. If not for the help of two experienced Pemon porters, we'd have been wandering lost on our own, swallowed from sight — *The Lost World*, indeed.

I'll never forget the sensation of waking the next morning, scratching inflamed welts on my legs as I stretched cold, wet socks onto my feet and jammed them into leather hiking boots stiff as pottery. Throwing open the tent flap, another planet stared back. An eerie world populated by surreal rock formations that looked like potato elephants, melted chess pieces, and mammoth charcoal-colored mushrooms. Between the crags and crevasses, ponds of water gleamed. Atolls sprouted from the pools displaying nests of flowering succulents.

Not far from our campsite we gathered in a snow-white field glistening with nuggets of quartz crystals. Looking spent but purposeful, the Oracle ambled to the center of the circle and brought through three successive beings, the Master, a Time Being, and the spirit of the Mountain itself.

You made it and I am smiling. I want you to please breathe from your diaphragm and connect to your third [chakra]. You'll find that your solar plexus's are rather on fire at this moment. The kundalini is quite high. If you were very good you could have warmed your clothes all by yourselves. Now I'm going to have the crystals thrown at me. I know you are all tired but running your energy will warm you up a bit.

This mountain is a huge crystal, and it is crystals that regulate time on this planet. And this is one of the few crystal mountains that have been untouched until recently. It's not very happy about it either. It doesn't like humans on it. This was not meant to be a living place. This is a place where life comes from. This is a place where time comes from. There are other areas that also helped construct timing in different ways. But this is the core area.

Liquid Time and The Kiss of God

The Master informed us this was the place the Godhead first kissed the planet. Where liquid time, the essence of the Godhead, touched solid time. Water met rock and together they created life.

You will feel the kiss in your third chakra. The integration of your soul and body, of bringing the two together and working together as companions. They are actually combining their forces so that they can create life.

Your body is the solid time; your soul is the liquid time. If [they] become separate, then evil and good are let go; they're let free so evil can do destruction. We describe evil by a force that loves to do harm. And because your souls have been so disconnected from the body for so long, evil has been allowed to be creative.

TIME BEING

The crystals have set up a timing on this mountain different than any other place. Here liquid touches solid all the time. Those two are always connected, and life can even happen on a rock like this, on a barren mountain like this. This is highly unusual. So feel the place in you where you can touch your soul and your body together.

We were asked to hold hands and connect to the mountain under our feet.

Now we are bringing in very minute dosages of this time element so your bodies are not hurt. Please understand we have set these equations up and have no idea what it's going to do. We've never done this with solid bodies before. If it's too much for your bodies, then try to release it. Your bodies are going to be little planets. And you're going to receive the kiss and create life, but we don't know what kind. Just as the Godhead, when it kissed this planet, didn't know what kind of life this planet would create. It has been re-creating forms over and over and continuing the life sequencing into better and better developing bodies.

MT. RORAIMA

Time is far more complicated than anyone could ever know. The sequence of time, as I bring now to your bodies, is layers upon layers upon layers. If your bodies were more agile, they could go through each doorway and see whole dimensions happening. I'm in each dimension of this planet like you see me now. This is very rare. Wherever you will be, in all sequencing of time dimensions, you will see the physical surroundings changing. I will never change. Until this planet is dust, I will remain its core time place.

Standing in the bed of quartz crystals on the misty summit, I felt ignited by the energy exchange. My feet burned with a dry heat and my third chakra felt like it had been plugged into an electromagnetic current, a sensation that made me aware of my rigid and resistant places, where the flow was blocked, or silent.

MT. RORAIMA

You will let energies in that can stop what is happening to this world. Energies you will not see or hear, but they are real and they will come through your body now because I have entered.

It became more apparent later how in order to open our third chakras it was essential for us to readjust the timing in our bodies, much of which was linked to the tightly measured handiwork of our watches and clocks. This is ironic because these mechanisms use quartz crystals to maintain their tick-tick, minute-to-minute precision; whereas, the energy we received on the crystal mountain of Roraima was given to us to help our bodies align closer to the rhythm and timing of the planet. A state of timing that would be further enhanced when we worked to increase the fluidity in our bodies at Angel Falls.

Just Shoot Me

The night's sleep was not enough to restore the Oracle's sore and weary body. The degree of swelling, pain, exhaustion, and emotional distress she had endured climbing the mountain made the descent even more difficult — skidding her down loose rocks, bracing and maneuvering her body around boulders, finding footholds to lower her where the path dropped sharply, and balancing her front and back where we crossed slurries of mud and water.

At one point, the Oracle turned to us and said, "Just shoot me." Soon after making this statement, she was taken out.

Maria came in and assumed control of her body. "Maria" is the name given to identify a strong and steadfast guardian being who is primed to enter the Oracle's body the moment trouble appears. This might come in the form of someone consciously or unconsciously getting into the Oracle's space, someone displaying threatening or hostile energy or, in this case, where her body has hit its limit — in other words, anytime she is in a stressed, emergency situation yet still needs to go on. When this occurs, a protective energy known as *Maria* comes to the rescue. Those who've been confronted by Maria never forget the impact. It feels like you're being embalmed with ice. Your aura contracts and your faculties freeze. Maria's chilling force can fill an entire room.

As we descended the mountain trail, we could tell Maria had entered the Oracle's body by the telltale absence of humor, the singular focus of her physical energy field, and the forceful tone of her voice.

We knew her body would crumble but we did not know how much it would crumble. We also knew we had Maria — in the sense that Maria would make sure her body would get down. Maria dictates quite nicely.

But even with Maria asserting the extra strength and endurance necessary, it was clear the Oracle's body had reached a critical state needing immediate medical attention. As we cleared the overgrowth near the base of the mountain, we heard the whirring propeller blades of a helicopter. It was a *deus ex machina* moment.[10] Called in by the tour company, the helicopter landed in an open field at the base camp and lifted the Oracle away to the nearest clinic in Santa Elena.

10. Deus ex machina, from the Greek: a person or thing that appears or is introduced suddenly and unexpectedly and provides a contrived solution to an apparently insoluble difficulty.

Personally, I could have collapsed right there, a wrung out, emotional wreck, but we needed to keep going. As we hiked on, relieved the Oracle was in helpful hands, my tent-mate and I jabbered about constructing a sedan chair with a cushioned throne and hiring four muscle-bound hulks to transport the Oracle on future trips.

We camped that night at the Kukenan River, where we were fed heaping plates of spaghetti while fireflies brightly flickered around us in the darkening savannah air. When we finally got back to Paraitepui the next day, my feet were tattered rags, bloodied with busted blisters. My arms and legs were pocked with festering bites, and I had puffy eyes and aching joints. We gave clothing and boots to the Pemon Indians in thanks and set off.

The Oracle met us later in the day in Santa Elena. She was beaming, and although she was swollen and aching from the climb, she was rested and much improved. She was not conscious of how she got down the mountain. She didn't even remember the helicopter. The only thing she recalled was being laid on a metal gurney and seeing a doctor, who — after listening to her heart with an antiquated EKG machine — told her she had the healthiest heart he'd ever witnessed.

Venting in Canaima

We flew to Canaima, where we were greeted by the thirty-eight other students who'd come for the next two weeks of travel in Venezuela. Seeing us, one related how we looked "like refugees from a war zone." We might have appeared worn down, but internally we were revved-up, supercharged by the energies given to us by the crystal mountain. In a later circle, we'd be relieved of this extra energy when it would be transferred hand-in-hand to the new arrivals.

Soon after reuniting with the others, those of us who had climbed Roraima sat with the Teacher to shed some grievances from our travails on the mountain, which needed to be expressed and resolved. Some were angry about being so ill-prepared for the ordeal and the wear and tear it took on the Oracle.

Do you know how hard it was to keep you alive? Let me whine a moment.

The Teacher reminded us of his prior warning about the difficulties we'd encounter and his promise that even though many of us had been slaughtered there in a prior life, this time we would come out alive.

The Mountain was testing you. It wanted to make sure that you had to work your utmost to get there. It threw everything at you. You were a very slow group, but you were also going through some enormously heavy time dimensions. Please understand we had it as set up as best we possibly could with all your karma levels. Unfortunately, I am not the one who gave you all your karma.

The reason we only did one trance up there is that [the Oracle's] third chakra was ready to rupture. We got the energy into your bodies. That was our major goal, and your kundalini would be set with it. Your thirds are spinning in a very different way. More whole, more round. It is moving in accordance to your planet now, in the same axis and rotation according to your sun.

Breaking Agreements

Taking leaves a wound.

In a later circle, it came up how a few people had picked up quartz crystals from the top of Roraima. The Teacher was appalled.

The agreement was to keep all the crystals on Roraima. They must go back. The agreement was very clear. This is said without judgment, but this is very bad. The promise was made that nothing would be taken. That was made directly to the mountain. What was in your minds and in your hearts? If agreements are made with these areas you must be very careful not to break them. You come into that exact same karmic level of arrogance in which you are trying to stop. Those crystals were taken in a lie. They were taken in self-entitlement and in narcissism. If you have to walk back to that mountain, they must go back.

There it was, a perfect exhibition of self-entitlement physically performed for all of us to feel. Crystals pocketed off the summit. The taking without asking, acted out from our solidity, and the ruins of our third chakras. These were not large crystals; they could fit in the palm of a hand, perhaps picked off the ground as a mere memento, a souvenir to bring home. But when it comes to nature, or in this case a mountain, there is no measurement. Stealing is stealing. It's about the energy of the action, the theft, not the size or the quantity of the object stolen.

Even one person taking something does harm and harms the work being done by the group. The land does not see you as one person; it sees the whole group.

Leaving Canaima, we motored up the Rio Carao in a couple of boats en route to Autantepui. When we reached the Churun River, we changed over into several long, dugout canoes. The river at this time was abnormally shallow. There were stretches where we had to get out and walk along the rocky banks to lighten the load, as river guides pushed and pulled the canoes up river to deeper water. Two of the canoes capsized en route, spilling folks into the river.

As we neared our destination, a number of us couldn't take our eyes off some tall monoliths of stone perched atop a tepui. They looked like four sentinels inspecting the intentions of whoever entered the home of Salto Angel, the highest waterfall in the world. The natives called the stones "witnesses." One person noted, "This is the first time I have felt physically looked at by a rock." The Oracle called them guardians, "magnificent and scary, watching our every move."

They've been eyeing you for quite a while. Especially since you came up river. They are quite strong. They can cause a great deal of trouble. They are there to make sure that people don't come.

Many of us frolicked in the clear pool at the foot of the sky-high waterfall. The misty spray from its massive splash undulated in the air above our heads. Still weak from climbing Mt. Roraima, the Oracle didn't make the hike from the river up to the pool, so we circled around her in the trees near the river with bottles and canteens of the Angel Falls' water she said we'd need.

The Law of Fluidity

The spirit of Angel Falls came in and told us it is not actually the tallest falls in the world, as assumed, but there is one behind it that is taller and mightier. The spirit of the falls had us pour the water we'd collected from its pool over our heads.

ANGEL FALLS

Now we must begin the connection of water to flesh. This is the beginning of a baptism. Water has always been the source. All creation has come from this source of life. It is very, very strong. The strength is in the fluidity, not in the power. It is not in the aggression. It is in the fluidity. I want you to touch this strength of fluidity now. You kill fluidity with your thoughts of what must be, your rules. You kill fluidity with your laws that don't apply. I want you to touch the strength of fluidity and know the law of fluidity. Touch the law. I'm putting it in front of you.

Angel Falls

The law of fluidity is the law of all and one. It is the waterfall; it is the river. It is all that can be given and all that can be received. The law of fluidity can only be received in connection. Where you are not connected, even though you are touching, you will not receive the law. Let the water connect you.

Connection, Connection, Connection

If there's one word that single-handily symbolizes the heart of the Teacher's instruction it is "connection." From the earliest of classes, this word has been drummed into us, with an emphasis on seeking and maintaining healthy connections that touch us in caring and compassionate ways, so we can come out of our dark and unconnected places to feel and gain more of who we are. We cannot grow and become whole alone. Isolation perpetuates the disconnection of body and soul. The Teacher has made it plainly clear, "Isolation is a killer." We need the caring and nurturing of others to reach our fuller selves. We need to let the outside world in without losing our identity in the process. This takes courage and honesty.

Connecting with places on the Earth is similar to person-to-person contact. True connection means bringing your caring, your respect for another's life, and your heartfelt intention to connect in a giving and receptive manner. It means looking and listening beyond your eyes, your ears and your beliefs without judgment. If undamaged, the spirit of the place will sense the expression of your energy field and connect back.

Connection has been described to us in numerous ways: as a creative act, as the key to consciousness, and as the path to being one with everything. As we stood around the Oracle under the canopy of the rainforest at the base of this towering waterfall, the meaning of connection was articulated in a new way — water's way.

ANGEL FALLS

Each drop makes a river. Each drop makes a falls. If one drop jumped out and said, "I don't wish to be connected. My life is my own. I am disconnecting." It would dry up, and by its own death it will bring death to the river, too.

This is the original baptism — the law of fluidity. All must begin together. All creation begins in the connection.

One thing that stood out as odd about the jungle around Angel Falls was the lack of bird song, animal noises, and insects. You would think such an abundance of water and vegetation would host a riot of critters. Instead, no sounds rippled the air. It felt mute, choked off. Of course, the absence of insects was a relief, but at the same time eerily abnormal for a rainforest. We came away thinking the area had been sprayed with pesticides, DDT or some other toxin, to spare tourists the annoyance of being a meal for bugs. The lack of sound in the area mirrored how the Master described our third chakras:

Your third chakras were murdered, killed, flattened, squashed in silence. They lost their sound. And where there is no sound, there is no growth.

When asked what we would be like if our third chakras were open, alive, and healthy, the Oracle responded, "We would relate to every creature on this planet and let them relate to us. We would not slaughter or cause extinction. We would care and acknowledge all the animals, the trees, and the waters. For us to be healthy we would have to help them be healthy. We would begin to understand what happens if we cause harm. We seem to know what we need, but we don't look at the needs of others. We would not have this greed. We would know what our actions mean to other life forms, and that if we harm life we harm ourselves."

Meeting the Yanomami

A couple days later, after failing to reach a site due to a heavy downpour and eating roasted guinea pig at a farm carved out of the jungle, we flew to Puerto Ayacucho. The flight filled our eyes with a breathtaking spectacle as the aircraft orbited one majestic tepui after another. The Oracle noted how, "Each tepui had its own sound, its own voice, its own soul." Long, silver strands of waterfalls sparkled in the sunlight around every turn as they plunged and disappeared into the dense forest below — which one traveler aptly described as "an unbroken mass of broccoli." Upon landing, we were driven to a camp along the Orinoco River where we lodged in huts.

One morning, half the group boarded a small plane chartered to fly us to La Esmeralda, with the intention of meeting a tribe of Yanomami natives. The other half of the group would fly there the following day. Along the way, our guide and pilot decided we would have a better chance of meeting the Yanomami if we flew down the Orinoco River to a settlement there. We didn't know at the time that this impromptu diversion was illegal.

The prop plane landed in a rough, grassy airstrip near the Ocamo River. I happened to be walking with the Oracle from the aircraft to the Yanomami meeting place. Along the way, I could sense the Oracle's energy field clinging to me. She was feeling the natives eyeing her from the trees. "They want me," she exclaimed. She wasn't joking. "They're making plans to keep me here with them."

Given the spur-of-the-moment, midair decision to land at this spot, I wondered how the Yanomami could possibly know who the Oracle was. Men, women, and children from the tribe gathered around us in a small open-air shelter under a thatched roof. They didn't appear to be at all surprised by our arrival. Days later, when asked how the Yanomami knew we were coming, the Master said he had appeared to them as a bird.

I told them you would be coming with a large white woman. That she was your shaman, your chieftain, although she is not your chieftain, but that is what they would understand. [I told them] we're preparing for them to be able to move into another dimensional time frame that [is] needed for the Earth. If the people outside of their world were going to learn to take care of the Earth correctly, they would have to teach them. So, would they please give the equations that would help teach them [us].

The purpose of meeting the Yanomami was to be in the presence of a people whose souls were of the Earth. Their souls come from the soul of the planet, much like the Aborigines; whereas, our souls are etheric.

Instead of the soul on the outside world, theirs is the inside world. They have a soul like the redwood trees have a soul, like the river has a soul. Many people call them animal-like. But they have intelligence, they have language, they have love, they have hate. They have all the emotions your bodies have, and they have [them] in a mature way. They know how to live and not destroy.

One could say they are Earth People, and we are Sky People, without any superior importance applied to either. They live in the physical, connective state of *We*, which is different from the etheric *I AM* state. The We is the physical body's inherent connectivity with all life forms. Living in the We, there is no "me" or "I," only us. The Yanomami have no word for being alone. The We is the unifying energy field the beast embodies in all the families of creatures on the planet. Nature does not perceive any one of us individually or single us out, but views entire species together — flocks of birds, schools of fish, and herds of elk.

[The We state] means that you are aware of your physical self so much that you are aware of [your] impact physically on all life forms around you, and your intent is clear, and the action follows intent.

What's interesting is how in the We state, and only in the We, each person experiences his or her own uniqueness, like single, one-of-a-kind snowflakes among the falling snow.

Our primary work in visiting the Yanomami was to exchange energies and receive their equations.

You're looking at one ancient group. These Indians carry the equation of the Earth. They carry the equation of life and death simultaneously in their bodies. They can live within the planet's system, without greed, [and not] with emotional harmony, but emotional honesty. And they are clear that they're moving into extinction. But before they go to extinction these equations have to go somewhere.

The Teacher also mentioned how the Yanomami might not like us.

In fact they may even view you with hostility. Because they know you [Western civilization] are going to be their killers, there's no reason to like you.

I felt more curiosity than hostility from these natives. It was a strange and intense sensation standing among them, far different from any experience I've had visiting other countries with foreign languages and traditions. Surrounding us was a group of barefoot, rainforest tribal people, whose bodies exuded strength, agility, and a heightened awareness of their environment that was far more heightened and grounded than mine. The short, wiry shaman of the tribe bonded with the Oracle and gave her a large parrot feather as a gift of their meeting.

"They smelled like earth," was the Oracle's first impression. "They were not only of the forest — the forest was inside them. No separation. They let us see that and touch it."

In terms of sharing their Earthly equations with us, we didn't ceremoniously hold hands, but something was exchanged body to body simply being in their presence.

"It was a privilege to stand among these people," a fellow traveler related to me. "Seeing them has to be one of the highlights of my life," another recalled. "I felt totally complete after being with them."

Before leaving their village, some of the men in our group traded with the shaman and others of the tribe for their long bows and arrows, which had been crafted to shoot parrots and wild game, while the women traded for handmade baskets.

There was also some dickering for the Oracle. Translated into Spanish by a man who was fluent in our group, the Yanomami wanted to know what we'd accept in trade for the Oracle.

It turned out our visit to the Yanomami village stirred up trouble. When the plane landed at the airport in Puerto Ayacucho, some soldiers from the army were waiting for us on the tarmac. The local officials were understandably angered by our visit. Although it was the Venezuelan guide and pilot's snap decision to fly to that Yanomami village, the over-riding concern of indigenous support groups and anthropologists was for the health of the tribe and the possibility of foreigners bringing disease.

Touching Beast along the Orinoco

The water plummeting down the high walls of the tepuis collects in streams that course through the jungle and feed the Orinoco River, inflating it into a surging mud-brown, mile-wide torrent, plowing its way to the sea. Frogs were croaking along its banks as we gathered on a rock outcropping near the river and listened to the Master speak about the current state of our beast.

The level of third chakra work with the beast is done energetically within the grounding that you're in. The area you're in, it's beast heaven. Earth's physical life is stimulating your beast. The third chakra is physical. In connecting the beast and giving beast back its reality, and giving it back its life, is about physical movement. The problem is you have a beast that's been solid and asleep for a long time.

Asked about the fatigue some were feeling, the Master replied:

It's everything the beast is feeling. You know if you were kept in prison for how many years and you were let out, wouldn't you feel anguish, despair, and anger? Your beast is feeling its anguish.

The beast can develop if its needs are provided. It cannot change from what it is. It will still be part of the planet. It will not view your souls as gods. Your souls will not be its gods. The plants, the rocks, the trees — those are its gods. Is that clear?

Your soul perceives the beast as an object. Not as a life form. If it comes through the genetic entity, it is the genetic entity that will teach it its life form. I want you to go into the beast structure. I want you to observe how it can receive.

I'm bringing in the area's beast to touch your beast.

BEAST OF THE AREA

In the earth we speak... hmmm... we speak in tones of life. We speak in tones of death. But we are not double like you. You speak the truth and you speak a lie in the same moment. You say "I care" and "I want" in the same breath. I don't know if I agree with your teachers that you can be caring and not wanting. I believe their hope is greater than your reality. So much rage to wake up something that should never have been sleeping. So much anguish for all the wrong. I hope your teachers are more correct. I will touch the beast in each of you. Happily. But will you crush it with a kiss again?

We stepped up to the Oracle's body one at a time and gave our ancient names. These ancient names are like verbal codes that re-touch the lives when we were more whole. The character of each person's beast at that time was described to them. Where one person's beast had strength, another's sought more life. Where one beast was in turmoil, another's sang.

In leaving, the Beast of the Area said, "Do not lie anymore. Please speak with the hands, not just the mouth."

Karma in the Jungle

Karma is a path not a prison.

Our last days in Venezuela were spent running energy as the Master touched each person and told them about their past lives in the rainforest and the tepui region. Some had once been healers; some had been artists, hunters, and shamans. These were lifetimes when we knew the Earth as a living being, and we communicated with mountains and with birds. We lived in communities where there was no single ruler. Everyone ruled. Some had once been water-bearers, with the facility to look into water and see the future. We'd also had lives as conquerors — the ones who'd murdered the natives — as well as past lives as natives who murdered those who brought change. The tragedy, beyond the carnage, is that our third chakras were sacrificed. The integration center between our bodies and etheric souls was shut down.

For many of you the karmic piece that you are touching at this moment is that destructive arrogant level. There's a tremendous self-entitlement piece among many of you, and I don't just mean you in this group, but many of you on the planet, that says, "I get to do this. I know I made this agreement but oh, no one will mind."

In a later session, the Teacher reiterated the destructive karma that had been created when human beings went solid.

When the connection was broken, the soul said, "Everything on this Earth is for me."

So what you have is a force of energy on this planet that wants to destroy it because it thinks it possesses it. Because humans believe they possess [Earth], they can do anything they want. They forgot that they're connected to everyone, connected to all life forms. They have grown ignorant of the fact that they need the trees to be alive, the plants, the rocks, and the crystals — alive.

One of two things will happen to your planet. The planet itself will die, or all humans will die because your planet will extinguish what is killing it. It will make you extinct. Nature will prevail.

Inspection Trips

Months before each trip, the Oracle would travel to the country to scout the places the Librarian had pinpointed for us to go. These locations were quite precise. Some were known sacred sites; others were off the spiritual pilgrimage path. Some were chosen for the energy they radiated, which would assist us in our connection with the planet and help open and develop our chakras. These were places where the Earth was willing to work with us. Other places were selected for their initiatory potential and because they emanated an energy that would help better blend our bodies and souls; some were places we could retrieve something we'd lost, touch a past life, and/or resolve painful karma. In some instances, the energy radiating from the land was unwelcoming because it had been damaged and needed a caring connection to help it heal. Occasionally, the site marked on the map where the Librarian stuck a pushpin would be unreachable, without road or trail, too perilous, or so remote the hike to and from would eliminate our chances of traveling to other designated sites on our prescribed itinerary.

These scouting trips also gave the Oracle a chance to meet the guides and touch the spirit of the land. Upon her return, she would set up a Teacher lecture to inform us about the work ahead and the purpose of the upcoming journey. Many of these pre-trip lectures included beings and energies the Oracle had encountered while traveling the region. The beings would help prepare us for what we'd be experiencing on our travels.

The Figure 8 Energy Pattern

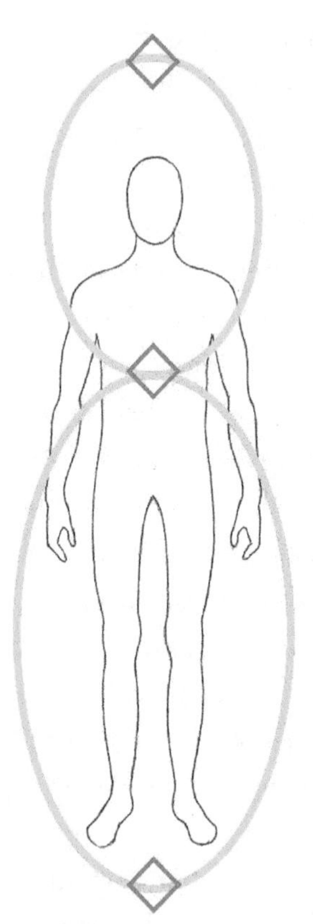

In classes after returning home from Venezuela, we were directed to circulate our energy in a figure 8 pattern.

This 8 pattern involves running a complete loop of energy from the eighth chakra below our feet to the third chakra and on up through the ninth chakra above our heads and back around.

This 8 pattern is a stable, circulating structure that extends our energy field and helps us become more conscious of the inside and outside worlds. It is foundational in the work of blending soul and body.

The Teacher said this is one of a number of geometric patterns we could run. It's an energy pattern that was practiced long ago in the Middle East.

We began by picturing the figure 8 in our minds and feeling the energy touch these three chakras. We needed to be heart-centered, grounded, and focused in present time as we learned to open up and allow the outside world to be as it is, without blocking or judging the sounds and activity around us. The figure 8 helped us connect to all the life around us. With ongoing attention and practice, running the figure 8 pattern became second nature, and we could simply call on it and allow the body to work it.

Although this image depicts a two dimensional loop, it later became three dimensional — moving more like a double eggbeater.

Looking out a Cave in Qumran

Israel

The most evil have walked this place and the most godly have walked this place.

The vigilant state of Israel became immediately apparent upon landing in Tel Aviv. The presence of rifle-bearing Israeli army women at the Ben Gurion airport was the first sign. Being pulled out of the customs line and escorted to a small room with "Ministry of Defense" tagged on the door was the second. The name in my passport — one of the most common names in the United States — had hoisted a red flag on their terrorist watch list. After a face-to face interview, they let me enter the country. Welcome to the heart of the world, land of messiahs and prophets; for centuries, a crossroads of cultures and conflict where covenants are born.

The year was 1993. The Teacher had planned this and subsequent travels to the Middle East fully aware of the optimum times our lives would be least at risk, safe from bombs and the clashes of combative factions. He promised none of us would die on these trips — joking how he didn't want any of us on his side. Seventy students had come to Israel with the Oracle to help open the heart chakra of the planet, and the heart chakra of our bodies, as well. We would meet a warrior, a prophet, and we'd revive an essential part of our spiritual selves that had been buried long ago.

The heart chakra is the conscious center of the body. In order to have a conscious body, you have to feel what you're feeling and own it. What Israel, the heart of the world, is going to say to all your hearts is, "Grow up." The old covenants are going to be changed. Not necessarily broken, because they [have been] built upon. They're not worthless, but they're old, and the new ones are going to start coming in. Your bodies will have to begin to stretch toward those.

The land of Israel emanates strong kundalini, which is a core fire energy of the Earth. The initial plan was for us to visit Hebron. We'd been told it was the place Abraham had come to from Ur in his search for the energy of the planet's center fires. This is also the place where Abraham and his wife Sarah had been buried in a cave. Unfortunately, our visit to Hebron had to be nixed due to recent hostilities there.

Qumran and the Essenes

On the northern edge of the Dead Sea lies the ancient settlement of the Essenes, a once fanatical subset of the Jewish nation, who some Biblical historians claim to have lived between the second century BCE and the first century CE. This group intentionally isolated themselves far from others in order to do highly concentrated spiritual work, which they felt would be corrupted if undertaken within society. Some of their writings, known as the "Dead Sea Scrolls," were discovered in caves in the limestone cliffs around Qumran in the 1940s and '50s.

Prior to our trip to Israel, the Teacher delivered a lecture about the Essenes, which I've edited and divided into three sections: The Essenes, the Teacher of Righteousness, and the Four Pillars.

The Essenes

Spirituality in those days was a very rigid thought form and very fanatical. Many of the groups in those time periods were concrete and fearful of losing their gods, and [they] would fight great wars for their belief system. There are still great wars being fought over belief systems, which from our side looks a little strange, because a belief system that is innately you — why would you fight over something that you already have?

The Essenes were not warriors. They did not have swords. But they were warriors with mathematics, sound, and their ability to create timing. This group of people was very involved with time. They were in recognition that their bodies were very solid and that they had to come back to God. But they first had to come back to their soul. In order to do that they were going to have to understand another level of timing. They were going to have to get out of linear time into spatial time.

One of their firmest beliefs was that time became fixed and stuck in the bodies.[11] *Their bodies stopped time, and that's what created solidity. And because time stopped in the body, then you couldn't*

11. "Stuck in time" or "fixed time" refers to how past traumas and pain can keep us fixed to these times, to experiences that caused us to hide parts of ourselves, which hold us back, unable to grow beyond them. Those who are not stuck in time might still encounter harm, feel pain, and cry, but they are not bound to the past; they transcend it.

know God because God was fluid. God kept moving. This was their belief. If the body was holding up the soul because it was stuck, and you had to live with this body, then it was important to bring in people that could un-stick your bodies. If they were a part of society, then they would have to live by the timing of society. They would never know spatial time. So they removed themselves.

The Teacher of Righteousness

There was a very special teacher of the Essenes. Your books call him the Teacher of Righteousness. This was a phenomenal person. He was unique in that he did not reject the rest of the world. He brought the world to the Essenes. The people who were connected to the Teacher of Righteousness had to study Judaism and many of the mystical and pagan religions. They did not have idols but they understood those religions, very carefully so.

The Teacher of Righteousness formed many of their rigorous levels, gave them what they knew to be true, and then was killed. He also gave them a great deal of identity, a great deal of ability to be on their own. They could, as a group, stay very strong.

It was only through the souls beginning to learn how to be with the body could they learn how to be with the planet and not do great harm. They knew that if tremendously evil forces could kill this planet, they could kill other planets and do great harm.

The Four Pillars

They [Essenes] began bringing in four children — the Four Pillars — children that could actually begin to change the planet by their mere presence. These children would be so special that God would speak through their bodies. This was their belief.

Three men and one woman were born in such a way that they carried no sin. They carried complete fluidity. One of them was Jesus.

Jesus was not supposed to be here by himself. Because [of] the volume of work, one person could never do [it all]. They brought in four children to begin the formation of changing physical time. [It's] very much what the planet's trying to do right now. It's trying to upgrade its vibratory rate.

For them to bring in a child that was fluid was an amazing feat. They could raise the vibratory rate around a pregnant woman [such] that her body never once knew fear, [and so her] child would be born without fear, without despair. The body did not know solidity. "That it would never leave the ocean," would be the words of the Teacher of Righteousness.

They were mostly celibate, but they actually picked people to have children. Joseph and Mary, for instance. It was not immaculate conception. They were pure in the sense that they knew both their light and dark sides. They understood themselves so completely that their bodies could generate enough time and fluidity that they could create a body with more fluidity, [a] body [that] was more soul-like also.

Jesus had a superior body because it wasn't stuck in time. He was not stopped by his devils, his demons. He was not part of the rest of the world whose bodies were stuck in time. Which means his soul could touch his body — which, as many of you have been complaining to me, "Why don't I know what my soul is saying to me?" He knew openly. His body could receive the soul's essence almost immediately, even before the age of seven.

Their biggest fear was to make sure that these children did not get involved with the society, especially when they were young. "Society will contaminate you."

They were saying: "We will bring in the Four Pillars. We will bring in energies from the four points of the universes, and we'll bring in such dynamics of energy that evil will die on this planet. We will be rid of all evil."

This is a level of beginning to bring in bodies that were so fluid, each with their own specific knowledge, that energy would come in and heighten the vibratory rate of the planet and the people on the planet. That meant they were directly challenging the main forces of evil. They were capable of carrying the Christ Force energy. * *It didn't mean they were without darkness. They had their dark side, but it was fluid. There is a difference between being evil and being dark.*

One [of the Four Pillars] carried timing — the main essentials of timing with the destroyer energy, not so much kindness, but of tremendous destructive force. Jesus came in love. He brought kindness, compassion, but also timing and healing. He brought tremendous healing to a very hurtful world, a world in despair that could no longer hear. Jesus carried more of the creative force and the other brought in the destroyer force. Destroyer and creator in the same room. It was hot! (!)

[Another] one carried the Life and Death level, meaning fire and water — of the integration in their body that anything they touch will be integrated. Another brought an extraordinary level of pure sound, beautiful voices of singing, beautiful songs of the angels.

Each one was an oracle, a prophet. The people around them were teachers, scholars. They were vessels. Even in their darkness they flowed. "We're bringing in the Godhead. We're going to integrate energies."

This is why they had four to bring in integration. One person cannot integrate. It's impossible. Integration is about many, it's about blending in the many in all levels.

[The Essenes] were seen as dangerous because they could keep evil from being able to function by integrating with it. One of the most challenging levels you [can] give someone that is evil is to integrate with it. It is to touch it, to remove it from isolation. If you ever want

to hear a harrowing scream and agony worse than you could ever believe to be true, watch a very evil person being touched.

The Teacher of Righteousness was killed by an extraordinarily evil priest, backed up with tremendous energies. The Teacher of Righteousness knew what he was doing and what he was challenging. That's why so much of the group could go on without him. They went on years without him and they functioned very well.

Many of the writings were happening at this time, very concentrated writings of the scrolls and hiding the information. A great deal of fear, not paranoia, but fear that it won't work. So many pressures were coming on them at this point, and they're carrying these four children who are enormously important to them. So they're feverishly writing. There are many more scrolls in those hills and caves than have been found.

Three of the pillars were killed before they reached their twenties. The woman is the only one who committed suicide, by the way. She walked off with the basic scroll of timing, and it is in a cave with her skeleton. It has not been found. This was all the universal secrets of time.

The Essenes were gearing up for a physical war when they were actually killed. They knew into their death that they had failed, and in that failure great wars would occur, that the massive amount of destruction that was happening etherically would happen physically, too, throughout the years. And it wasn't just them by the way. There were Polynesian groups. There were other groups in the orient also fighting the same level.

When the Pillars were killed, by the same person who killed the Teacher of Righteousness, [the Essenes] lost. They could not carry the energy. Together they could, they could hold. And mathematically they could actually keep energies, work energies, they could write numbers in the sand and create fire or have water. They could utter certain sounds and intonations and before them create a plant, a living plant. They could do this because they knew how to invoke the sounds of creation. They knew how to touch it and develop it and how to keep it growing. They didn't know how to do this as one person — they knew this as a group.

This is where you're not going to like some of this information. I'm sorry if it offends you. It is not meant to be offensive. It is simply what I know to be true. Jesus went out by himself and decided that he would still teach. Remember, he's living a life now where he's been under attack a great deal. By going out and teaching what he knew, Jesus truly felt he could bring about more than if he didn't do it. He was coming from an arrogant point of, "I can do it alone," even though the teachings said he could not. That chaos would be created if only one body went out. He felt that he and his disciples could do it. He did not understand that it was only one part of the universe. The four were needed to keep the balance. The other three were weeping.

Jesus could not keep chaos from taking over because he did not carry enough structure. This is true any time you make changes, or you're creating something new in your life, you [will] experience chaos. If you have enough structure, the chaos does not win over.

The Essenes could not hold the chaos down. They understood then that they were going to die. They agreed to die. And they knew when the soldiers were coming. They also agreed that they would disappear, that the ones with the greatest knowledge would go and would take with them all the laws they could. Even so, many of the scrolls were confiscated by soldiers.

Dying wasn't the worst thing that could happen to them. These people were thinking of lifetimes. They weren't thinking of just one lifetime. They were very clear that dying was really the better act to do because what they would live in was complete chaos. They really did die mischievously. Many of them died with a grin on their face. They weren't victims to their death. If you don't die a victim, you're not going to carry that fear into the next life are you? A lot of your fears came from other lifetimes.

Looking at what the Essenes attempted to achieve, the Oracle saw how it was not a single soul they were bringing through each body of the Four Pillars, but multiple souls. Each Pillar needed to carry a great amount of etheric energy with an extensive scope of dynamics to have the planetary impact they sought. For their goal to be actualized, all these souls would need to form strong agreements, not only with each other, but also with the Earth.

It makes you wonder what the world would be like today if the Essenes had succeeded.

The dry, golden land of Qumran felt gently enlivening to me. After walking a bit among the stonewall remnants of the Essene village and aqueducts, the group gathered around the Oracle in a secluded area away from tourists. We ran the figure 8 energy pattern we'd been practicing in classes as the Teacher of Righteousness came in.

TEACHER OF RIGHTEOUSNESS

We ask you to feel the energy of this place — the place where many of the laws were written and then hidden; where many of you were killed, and many of you laughed when the soldiers actually stuck a sword into your belly or cut your throat. You laughed right at their faces. Some of you prayed. Some of you spoke the laws to these soldiers. Some of you are the soldiers that the laws were spoken to, and then you knew the light. You could see it, you could feel it, you could see that path because the law was spoken to you.

The laws gave you structure because you did not know formlessness at all. You needed those laws, those words to have some kind of concrete knowledge and a path, but [it] was not a painted idol or doll; [it] was a word and a language you could speak. And as you spoke, it would come to you in meaning in your heart, and each spoken word would help open up each part of your heart and your limbs to the spirit of the law so you would not become lost. Because when a young one becomes lost they usually stray to what looks easy to them or known to them, and they will go where the many are because [it] looks more known to them.

Only the person with a heart will know that where the many are may not be for them. They will have to say, "No" to the many, or to that path that looks so much easier and so much more welcoming. They will sell their very souls if they must, so not to be alone. And in the days when I came there was so much work to do to help alter the energy and time of the planet, itself.

So, as we do this work, you have to understand that it's not just for the individual self, and it's not just for your group, it is for the Earth. Because you are beginning to bring the Earth to another dynamic.

Masada

From Qumran we traveled south to Masada, a high, solitary plateau overlooking the Dead Sea. In ancient times, some surviving Zealots and Essenes scaled Masada to escape Roman soldiers. They turned the palace of Herod the Great into an encampment, which kept them safe for three years. So determined to conquer these rebels, Roman legions built a huge ramp of stone and earth up the side of the mountain. As the ramp advanced to the walls atop Masada, the people had to choose whether to surrender and see their families turned into slaves, fight and die by Roman swords, or commit suicide. When the soldiers reached the summit ready to lay siege, they were met with silence. Before them lay more than 900 dead bodies.

Rather than take the cable car up the mountain, we hiked the "snake path" in pre-dawn darkness. The flat summit was eerily quiet, as if every hint of sound had been suppressed. A grim, heart-stopping feeling swept through me while standing on the western edge of the plateau overlooking the Roman's stony ramp, still there, seemingly undisturbed, as if the assault was still occurring. You could almost hear their voices, the rattle of armor, and the tramp of Roman feet storming up. A sudden boom rattled me back to the present moment as an Israeli fighter jet sliced across the sky overhead, breaking the sound barrier.

We circled in the ruins as the Oracle brought through the Teacher of Righteousness again.

TEACHER OF RIGHTEOUSNESS

In the desert and in the fire it is well advised to carry one's own water in order to bring in spirituality. Each [person] tested in the wilderness has been consumed by fire and had to learn to bring their own water or they died, dried out like a prune. That is what the desert taught them. In a way, it was not punishment. But it was harsh; they had to not speak or think. Their hearts had to be so open to not let the fire consume them. They had to bring in the waters of the universe at the same time the fire was consuming them. For those that could not find the ability to open their hearts, the desert could even dry out a soul — the fire was so intense. This is why this is the heart of the planet. The fire is most intense here. The kundalini is the most intense in all the world.

We were asked to run the figure 8 pattern and bring in the fiery energy that helped Abraham father a new nation — the same energy the Essenes radiated. The Teacher of Righteousness and other non-physical beings assisted us in working with this energy.

TEACHER OF RIGHTEOUSNESS

Now this is important, because the rest of the trip you will be running this energy. It is very difficult energy. This does not mean you know what you are doing, nor do we think that you are so spiritual that you are all masters. This means you are competent people in your world, many of you with your weaknesses, your hurts, and your strengths. You are not supposed to be perfect people. In fact, you are most imperfect.

Let the fire open every pore of your body, and with the mother and father energy allow the soul to enter with the open pores and open hands and openness. Do not let the thoughts be of what you can create. Let the thoughts turn to what is needed in creation. Enjoy the quality of the fire. Let it burn down some doors.

The mother and father energies the Teacher of Righteousness referred to are the builder and nurturer energies Abraham and his wife Sarah carried.

The Teacher of Righteousness left and an Essene came in.

AN ESSENE

Your paradise is not now in this lifetime. Your world is poisonous. Your lives have just begun to get exciting. Who you are is better than what we did. We were not warriors enough. You will be learning more about the warrior way.

As we moved from the city to the wilderness we made the mistake of thinking we could run from it and try to change it [by] being outside of it. It was incorrect. For those parts of you that have died, dying is fine, but it didn't complete the cycle.

The Essene explained how there were beings around us who would help bring the spirits of those who had died on Masada to those of us who'd lost our lives there.

AN ESSENE

There are ghosts here ready to come into your bodies, part of yourselves that need to come through. And you must bring them back with you.

In your heart and in your body and in your soul where there is lack of self, invite self in. Say hello to your self again and give that self food and water and warmth and comfort. Bring them to the fire and keep them warm. They have been cold without you for a long time.

Thank them for what they have done. They have enabled you to be free. Let them into the home that is a new home. Let them bring their books, let them bring their knowledge, let them bring all of their parts to you. They are children of light. Ask them what they need to feel welcomed and one with you. So much ripping apart, long ago and now. Let this mend and heal the rip.

The "ripping apart" the Essene alluded to is about how murder tears the connections between the soul, the body, and the Earth.

As the spirits of Masada were invited back, one of the men in our group wept uncontrollably. He later described his experience of reuniting with the man he'd once been on Masada as bittersweet — a feeling of joy for the reunion mixed with the pain and guilt of having to kill his family there rather than see them victimized by the Romans. The impact was so profound he began studying Hebrew soon thereafter, and later he converted to Judaism. "Because of that experience," he said, "I feel more complete in who I am."

The Heart of a Warrior

I always knew fear. It was always with me. It attended everything I did. It's stupid not to be afraid. It is more stupid to hate it.

Simon Bar Kokhba

We bussed through the Judean Desert and parked along the west side of the Dead Sea, where we hiked up Mishmar Wadi. As with so many of our ventures, we had no idea where we would end up, whom we would meet, and what we would learn. So, we packed food and water for the day and headed up this dry, desolate canyon into the unknown, until the Oracle stopped at the spot that told her, "This is it."

Not being a historian or biblical scholar, I was unfamiliar with Simon Bar Kokhba. Yet from the moment the Oracle began bringing him in, I felt I was in the presence of a fierce and formidable man. Later, I learned he had led a revolt against the Roman Empire in 132 CE, and for four years he fought and maintained an independent Jewish state, until the Romans finally crushed it.

Simon came in and asked us if there was water and wine. We gave him some water, which he drank with the Oracle's mouth.

SIMON BAR KOKHBA

I controlled a lot of people. I gave them solutions. The solution was to kill soldiers. The solution was to be free. They didn't know how to do it alone. No one ever does, you know. Everyone needs somebody to show them the open door.

You are weak. You haven't been tested enough. You haven't had to use your strength in places that are the most unpleasant — to endure actual emotional, psychological, and physical distress. You don't know yet what you can handle. You still love your passions too much.

I was never known for my tactfulness and pleasantries, and I'm not going to begin with you. (!)

Simon walked us through the three aspects of being a warrior.

First Aspect of a Warrior

You have to forget to wait for everything to come to you. You will have to say, "How do I walk to this?" Then, "How do I begin to change it? How do I bring my hands and my feet to this place? And what is the part I can change, and what is the part I cannot change that I must accept and comply with? And if I must accept and comply how much of myself must I sell?"

Did you know that even if you were to die trying to solve this problem you would be more alive than waiting for the problem to end? This is the first level of the warrior. You walk to the place where it is because what is weak in you will wait. It will wring its hands and it will cry and say, "I cannot, I cannot, I cannot." And what is strong in you will say, "Let me touch it, let me bring my sight to it, my ears to it, my breath to it, and my mouth to it, and let me bring it to a level I can handle and let me find the place that my breath comes to it."

And that is the warrior.

Second Aspect of a Warrior

"Is this problem worth solving or do I kill it? Do I remove it? Do I say it is too much? What is to be done with this?"

If it is not worth solving, kill it. If it is an emotional problem in you, then you must let an emotion die because it is no longer worthwhile keeping. There is no solution. You say goodbye to it. There are all sorts of ways of letting things die. Are you so inadequate in death that you don't know how to let something die? Warriors kill things all the time. They have to kill. That's what they do; they learn to kill and they learn to live. It's not always done with a sword, but it's always done with blood of some sort, even emotional blood.

Third Aspect of a Warrior

The action is in the beginning, it is in the middle, and it is in the finishing. [The warrior says], "I will bring my action and my choice to all stages. I will not let another shine a light and tell me what it is. I will bring my own voice and my own eyes to it. I will experience it myself. I will walk with it, and then I will decide what I must do."

Dolmen in the Golan Heights

Dolmens and the Death of the Human Soul

Let no bones be buried here, only the shadows of souls.

An Ancient

Our buses pulled to the side of the road in the Golan Heights of northeastern Israel for us to take photographs. Before us a hillside of grass blades tittered in the wind among blooms of tulips, narcissus, and hyacinths. As we stretched our legs, we were cautioned not to wander off due to the number of landmines that had been deployed by the Syrian army in the '70s. Above our heads, white storks rose in the thermals, kettling in high spirals.

A little later, we reached the Gamla region, where many dolmens had been erected. Dolmens are ancient stone structures made up of two or more upright stones that support — like the legs of a table — a huge flat stone, or capstone, on top. Commonly referred to as "portal tombs" or "portal graves," these monuments are said to have originated anywhere from 3,000 to 7,000 years ago. What's truly captivating about dolmens is how they're found all over, from Russia and the Middle East to Europe and the British Isles, with the most concentrated numbers showing up along the Korean Peninsula. All told, there are thousands of them dotting the Earth. Their meaning, and the people who built them, have long been a puzzling mystery. Speculation has suggested that nomadic tribes traveling the world made them. What adds to the mystery is how the builders were able to lift and position the enormous capstone slabs weighing upwards of a hundred tons.

We learned how these dolmens were not built as funerary chambers for deceased notables, but as gravesite monuments for the death of the Human Soul.

ANCIENT PERSON

It is a graveyard without a bone, because it wasn't bodies that died. It was the soul of the bodies that died. Not the souls of your higher selves. The souls of the bodies.

We were a people thousands of years ago who knew we were into a level of inside death. And we knew the mothering and fathering would be lost, forgotten; the women and the men would lose the Earth as their mother and father. We set up gravesites for you. These are your tombstones to losing your mother and father. Each one bears your name, of the world, of all humans.

Here is where we walked and understood we would go through many, many years of not knowing the Earth, of not touching the Earth.

Your purpose here today is to wake up this site. You will have to run energy and go to the past. So as you walk today, the land will release your human soul. In releasing the human soul, the land will begin to wake up and come join the life cycle. The human soul will touch the body and the etheric soul. And the etheric soul will join in the song of the human soul.

With your human soul encased in the planet, you could not know the touch of the planet. You were dead to it. You were buried to it. Your tombstones are here.

Now you will run fire. You will run the figure 8.

There were very old prayers prayed in a language far dead. It is not necessary to say those prayers now. We will make new ones now. The old prayers spoke of a death of many, many nations — of [the] continuing death of many, many nations to come. And that continuing death will occur for more years to come. It is imperative that the human souls can come back to the bodies that can stay alive and can create.

In this prayer that I speak, you must bring it in through your feet and you must let the wind carry it into your bodies. You must open your hearts, your minds, and all that you can to let the wind in.

Throw your biological parents away. Throw them to the wind and let the wind carry those parents away. And let the Earth be the parent. Let it speak through your feet to your heart and let your heart burn with the kiss of the Earth. Bring in the kiss. It must come to the heart. Through the eight. Through the fire. Through the caring.

And the [human] soul said that after all these years in the dirt, in the rock, "Will I know how to live in these bodies so solid?" And the Mother said, "You will learn. You will bring life back to the body and you will learn. Bring in the life of the planet and the winds and the rock and make it a gravesite no more."

At first, it seemed to be yet another subtle energy structure that we would learn to feel and invite into our lives — much like the triangular system — this one being a seed of the Earth's soul humans had once embodied. It wasn't until later we came to realize the transcendent attributes of the human soul and the magnitude of what we'd lost.

The Human Soul

The human soul is different from the etheric soul. Whereas a person's etheric soul comes from a far larger oversoul, the human soul comes from the soul of the planet. Mother Earth gives a particle of its soul to all its life forms. This particle of its soul is centered in the body between the second and third chakras.

The etheric soul connects to the human soul. The human soul is the combination of the genetic entity and the beast. It is a complete blending of the whole lower chakra system to the top chakra system.

Through the soul-to-soul connection of the etheric soul and the human soul, a more complete blending of the body and etheric soul can occur. As human beings became more solid, we began disconnecting from our human souls. We no longer sought its light, its consciousness and wisdom. This loss is evident in our perception and belief of being the superior species on the planet, which manifests in our narcissistic destruction of the environment around us.

The value of the human soul cannot be overstated. Without this particle of the Earth's soul alive in the body, our spiritual growth is stunted. We cannot bring more of our etheric souls into our physical bodies without a connection to this seed of the Earth's soul — a connection that brings consciousness of the world of spirit into more focus and clarity.

With their human souls, the ancient ones were able to sense and qualify the energy emanating from the land, perceive the planet's magnetic lines, descend into caves to hear the planets of the solar system speak, chart constellations, create extraordinary calendars, and much more.

All living things are not only expressing God from the etheric soul, but [they are] also expressing Earth from the Earth soul. The goal of the body is to express the Earth's life and to increase the life of the Earth. Every living body, every insect, every animal, every plant, every atom, every molecule, everything that comes from this planet, [has as] its sole purpose to express life in order that the planet can continually grow.

Reclaiming one's human soul is not an instantaneous act. It doesn't happen overnight or fully revive in a single lifetime. Abandonment feels no different for a human soul than for a human being. In our soul work, we've been assisted in retrieving our human souls through a number of guided energetic activities, all the while cautioned about the human soul's fragility. It can be easily diminished, broken, and killed by self-hatred, self-neglect, and narcissism. To bring it back to life takes caring and kindness to the planet in all its forms.

Many of the bodies I see are in despair and tremendous depression, not from what they've just experienced [in] this present life, but [because of] their disconnection from the planet and their inability to give back or to express the life because they can't receive the life from the planet.

The Old Cemetery

The Town of Safed is situated on a mountaintop north of the Sea of Galilee. It is well known as a spiritual center because many masters of the Kabbalah, the mystical theosophy of Judaism, lived and studied there in the sixteenth century and centuries before.

Our work directed us to Safed's old and famous cemetery located on a steep slope west of the town. Upon arriving, we quickly noticed how some of the standing tombs had been painted blue. Stepping among them, the Oracle was delighted to discover how alive the graveyard felt to her. Many of those buried there were revered rabbis and scholars. Although they've been dead for centuries, she could hear them still animatedly talking and debating among themselves. We would soon learn that what gave these dead such aliveness was in their bones.

DEAD RABBI

What are you doing here with a pile of bones? (!) *You know bones don't give wisdom. What can you do with bones that you can't do with anything else?*

They rejuvenate!

I have been here a long time. And look at how we helped to rejuvenate this area. Our land, our love. My bones and all these bones give always to the land. The secret of death is in the bone tissue. It does not die if you have a human soul. Only if you have a human soul [will] your bones be alive even when you die. Your skin will go. Your muscles will go. All that goes, but what's left behind are the bones.

The human soul belongs to the Earth. It is part of the bones. And in the bones is the rejuvenation of all life. If you could say the correct words, and these bones were alive, you could bring a person back to life [who has] been buried for hundreds of years. Did you know that? [No]

You are alive, your bones have not been dead for hundreds of years, have they? Does that mean you could start bringing more life to you? (Yes) Now, if you could do that with dead bones, can you do that with Earth? (Yes) But the bones have to be enough alive.

The Rabbi had us repeat after him: "I am a human soul with an etheric soul. And unto both we will become one. Inside the bone and outside the bone, unto the inside world and to the outside world, I will know both — not as an illusion, but with heart and with light."

DEAD RABBI

The greatest touching of all is at the moment of death between the human soul and the etheric soul. And the human soul gives to the etheric soul a message to God, and the etheric soul takes it and has knowledge of it. And the human soul takes the information of the etheric soul to the Earth. The etheric soul gives a message to the Earth, both thanking each other in a last caress before one is laid to rest and one flies away. That is death, in a caress, in a touching.

But if there is no human soul, or where there is a lie inside the bone, the soul cannot take the message to God, and the body does not lay to rest. It shivers in the dirt. It cries out. Nothing grows in that place. Nothing grows. Creation is stymied. You have a whole culture of graveyards where nothing is growing, and they are called your cities. They are non-human graveyards where everything is decaying inside and outside. And the soul from afar cannot come to bring light to it.

Sea of Galilee

History sprang to life everywhere we traveled in Israel. Our guide would direct our eyes out the window of the bus: "The field over there is where David slew Goliath." Then he would point to a hilltop and say, "That's where Samson was born."

One evening, a boat was chartered to take us out on the Sea of Galilee. The water was choppy and the boat tipped and tossed as we sat and stood on an open deck. We had no idea the Oracle would be bringing in the spirit of Jesus of Nazareth to speak with us, answer questions, and tell us a story about self-love.*

JESUS[12]

I was human. Both my parents were without karma, and that is the virginity you speak of. I wasn't a messiah in how it has been proclaimed. That was not my purpose. I claimed to be a prophet. I claimed to be son of God. I claimed to be the one which came to bring a message. I claimed many things. I also claimed that unto all, all could be like me, [and] that I was a son of light, [who was] here to talk with the sons of darkness, as all Essenes were. I proclaimed all could walk the path I was walking; all were children of God. All are messiahs. All are teachers.

Asked about Christ Force Energy, Jesus said:

It's only found in humans that are carrying human souls. You are now just beginning to touch it in yourselves. Only those who dare walk a spiritual path, only those who dare seek their shadow can bring in the Christ-force energy. Only those that can go to the wilderness and fight their devils can hope to touch Christ Force Energy. Before it entered, I had to fight my devils. And then I had to fight the world devils. I had to fight both, the inside devils and the outside devils. Only then did it come to me. Only then did it enter my body and begin to teach.

Asked about self-love, Jesus told us a story.

I once spoke of a flower that was in a desert where it was all salt. The flower started as a seed and the bird flew. It was a flower from this area where it was lush and green. In my day, this was all lush and green and the water was pure. And [the bird] flew to the very southern end of the desert and it dropped the seed. And the seed found itself in salt. Not in dirt, rich in nutrients or rich with moisture. It found itself in a surface of salt where the nights where so

---

12. Readers have every right to question (as some of us did) if indeed the spirit of Jesus was really speaking to us on the Sea of Galilee, but we didn't let that take away from the beauty of the message.

cold and the days so hot. And the seed buried itself as the sand moved across through the great winds. It still had great need to be alive and to bring life to the place where it was. Yet all around it was barren and [there was] nothing to nurture it so that it could be a creative flower and grow and be above the soil.

And it thought to itself, "It is still my need. Can I be a speck of beauty although it is nothing but sand all around me? And it is so barren, it has nothing yet to give me." And with the thought of its own creation and its own purpose to be a flower, nothing more but to be a flower, it stated its need to bloom. So when the sand blew over, it began to know warmth. It began to know the nurturing of the desert, not as it wished it was here in the north but as it was. And [it] said, "I receive what this desert has to give me because my goal is to be a flower."

So the seed took root unto salt and sand. It found in the root that there was water underneath and found the soil in which to grow. And within a few weeks' time, the flower grew above and was a royal purple flower that burst with beauty in such a way that within the whole desert this one moment of purple was there, beautiful and alive, and the flower understood that it had achieved its purpose. That it had found all the nutrients in the sense of what was there.

Self-love begins with the knowledge of what is your purpose and acknowledging purpose of self. Even unto a desert you must still achieve your purpose. Love is where you may achieve your purpose. And within that purpose, look around you. What are the nutrients? For in the purpose itself is your love. Your ability to achieve it is your love. And ability to express it is your love. And your ability to share it is your love. And your ability to give the seed to another bird to another part of the desert is your love.

And so that same flower, generations later, found itself again back in the north. But after that, it left a trail of flowers. Where, you see, the seed grew, and the desert grew with it. And because the flower's purpose was to be a flower, the desert began to know a flower. And the flower knew the desert.

Banias Spring

One afternoon, we hiked down the sunny hillside from Nimrod's castle past wild cyclamen and anemones to the clear, running headwaters of the Jordan River. We'd come to fill our bottles with the water of the river, which we would be carrying with us up Mt. Sinai at the end of the trip. A Teacher of the Waters came in through the Oracle and had us listen closely to the percolating song of the water at the spring.

TEACHER OF THE WATERS

All water comes from outside the Earth. It is not made here of the planet. It is from your outside worlds.

All the prophets, all the saints, all the messiahs went to the wilderness to find the soul of their body. To find the soul from afar, they came to the waters.

You are now seeking the fluidity of the body. As the water makes its sound, listen for the sound of the soul. If you enjoy this sound, then the sound of the soul is just as beautiful. It comes through the silver cord and makes as lovely a music as this bed of water does.

The Silver Cord

The silver cord is an etheric umbilical cord. It enters the body from the soul through the ninth chakra, and then it passes down to the seventh chakra at the crown of the head.

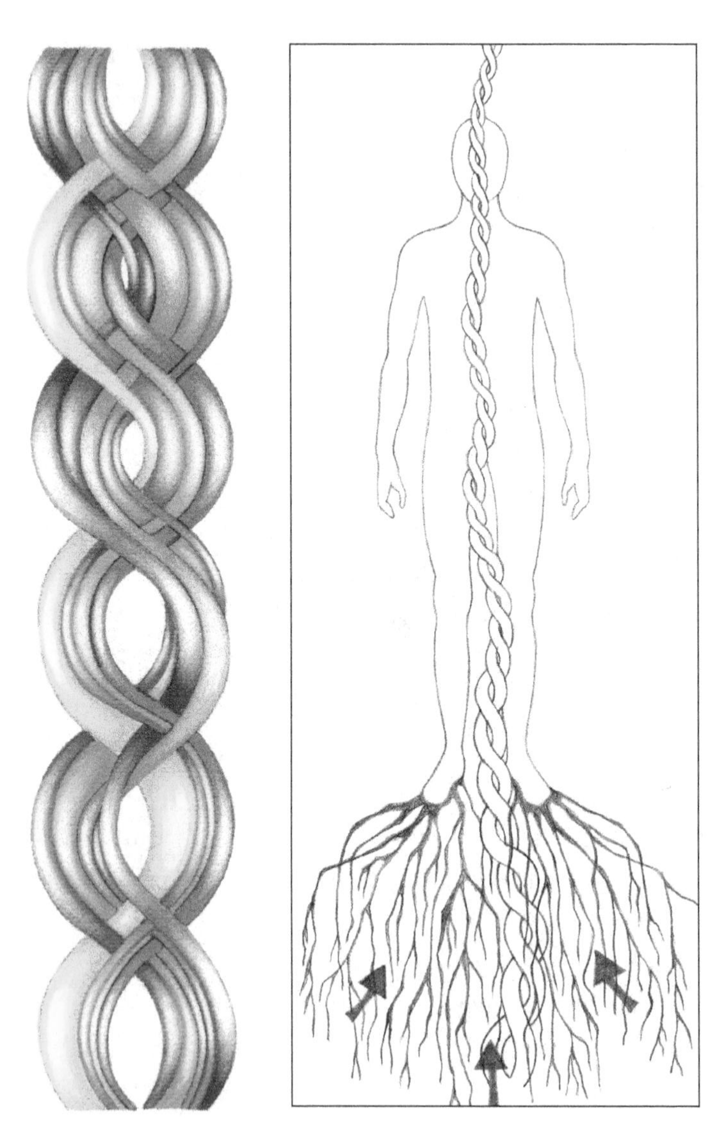

NOTE: The illustrations are simplified depictions of the silver cord. In actuality, the strands of the cord, of which there are thousands, are translucent, misty, and ever-moving. Although multi-colored, it has been called a "silver" cord, most likely because of the brilliant sheen it gives off when observed psychically.

The cord is not a solid form, nor is it silver. It is actually thousands and thousands of multi-colored strands of sparkling light consisting of mostly soul material. Knowledge is carried and exchanged through these myriad strands of light from your soul to your body, and from your body to your soul, all during your lifetime and through the time of your death.

The etheric aspect of the silver cord radiates with light like the tail of a comet. The physical aspect moves with sound. The truer the sound emanating from your body the stronger the light coming to you through your silver cord from your etheric soul. Depending on how connected the physical body is with the etheric soul, there can be a constant feeding of energy, or a minimal exchange carrying less color. The figure 8 energy pattern we circulate are made up of the strands of the silver cord.

These threads of soul light have been compared to a harp, which is interesting because it corresponds with the heavenly image of angels playing harps on clouds. The Oracle pointed out how clearly this harp image captures the separation of body and soul, and how in that belief, "You can only make music with your strands when you're dead."

It's possible to have dead parts in your silver cord, which are seen as solid and broken strands with no sound or light. In people who lack aliveness, the silver cord will have very little color. A truly evil person will have a thick, solid silver cord.

The silver cord is not something to tamper with or attempt to manipulate, heal, or direct in any way. We're not capable of changing it or improving it without harm. Self-entitlement and narcissism can harm it as well. We've been taught to leave it to our higher selves to work with it in a beneficial way.

TEACHER OF THE WATERS

Begin to move through the silver cord as you're listening to the water. Listen for your soul. Because the water will speak to you of your soul. Let the sound of the water guide the sound of your soul.

Now let the soul bring to you, in this sound, the purpose of your soul in this body. The silver cord is your harp, not your heart. So let the light play your harp and let your heart listen.

And I went to the desert to find my devils. And to meet them there, and to burn with them there. But I went to the waters to find my Gods. And it was in the waters that I found my Gods, one and many, one and all. And in the one there were millions of drops of water that made a river that began my life.

When asked, "Why did you find your devils in the desert?" the being said, "*Because evil cannot bear water.*"

This statement made me think of the iconic scene in the movie, *The Wizard of Oz,* when Dorothy flings a bucket of water in an attempt to douse the flames burning the straw of the Scarecrow. The water splashes on the wicked witch, who recoils, begins to steam, and then melts into the stone floor.

Capernaum

We traveled on to the north shore of the Sea of Galilee to work in ancient Capernaum, a place that emanated a luxurious, shimmering light. We walked among excavated stone ruins of an old synagogue and gathered on a mosaic floor open to the sky and in view of the gleaming Galilee waters.

The Master first spoke of Abraham and how he was a rare being, born a light soul with a human form and a human soul. He said we needed to be like Abraham so this kind of body would no longer be rare on the Earth.

When God said to Abraham, "I will make you many nations," he didn't say "Moslem, Christian, Jew, and Buddha." He didn't say this to him. He didn't say, "And this is what you must preach, and this is what they must learn, and this is what they must believe." He said, "Teach them my light and give them my name but not my face, so that inside them they will know who my face is. Into their own oneness I will come and touch the many in them and bring oneness to the many."

The Oracle later related to me how, "Good teachers don't tell you how to use the information they share. You'll find the purpose for the learning, make it your own and grow with it. There are no rules to learning. The rigidity of religion comes from men who have rules, not learning. Each person has to find their way to learn."

The Master left and the spirit of Jesus came in to speak with us once again.

JESUS

This land that you are in at this moment has always been sacred to many, many cultures and many generations. The waters have always been sacred because of their life-bearing properties. Water is always sacred for any life, for creation to grow. And you have water from the river. And with the water you must wash your hands when you are on the mountain [Sinai] and wash your feet on the mountain so you will be clean and the waters will give you creation on a mountain that has given you laws to allow you to create without chaos.

I was a carpenter. And I built beautiful tools, and beautiful things and furniture and wagons and wheels. And if I did not do this, my hands would become clumsy and I would become lazy. I would be a glutton for my laziness, for others to serve me. In my ability, in my ritual of building, and in my foundation that my father gave me, I made my building my own and I shared it with my father. My father no longer was my master nor was he over me. As I learned and grew strong in my craft, my father and I worked together not as master to slave, father to son, but as master to master. And so that is the walking with God, in a foundation given to you.

Asked about his resurrection, Jesus said:

I did not die on the cross. I did come back because I did not die. The death of the Christ Force left my body. And that was a death, yes, because the Earth knew not the Christ Force any longer. And so great harm could come. The man Jesus lived on as quite a normal rabbi because I was always pretty normal as a man. Knowledgeable, yes. And [I] brought new information, yes. I was a light being with a human soul. But the Christ Force left and that's what died on the cross. Humans killed the inside of themselves, and that's why great harm has come of Christianity, as much as good has come.

I carry on the responsibility of what my actions did, but not of the others. The Teachers that went after me and forced you to conform, those forgot my words. Nor were they my teachings. I said, "Go teach." I didn't say, "Enslave."

After the Oracle's trance, I was overcome with a giddy exuberance that could not be contained. My joy wasn't about the information we'd been given, it was the energy of the place that tickled me. And this buoyant radiance of Capernaum did not affect only me. Milling around the ruins with a few other men, our elation turned contagious. Soon we were revving so loud with laughter we were told by the officials to leave the grounds.

Sacred Sites

Not all sacred sites such as Capernaum bring out a joyous release. Every place is different and affects visitors in myriad ways and emotional responses, including everything from epiphanies of startling clarity and inspiration to ordinary, everyday states of being.

A sacred site never tells people what to be, but how to be. How they can be. But they don't want to listen to it, because that would mean they would have to change, or they would have to touch places in themselves where they would feel condemned or wrong. So a sacred site teaches us acceptance, not only what we can be, but who we are at the moment.

It helps to let go of all hopes or expectations when coming upon a sacred site. Be aware that the energy emanating from the land or a body of water is not there to make you feel good. However, in the exchange of touching and being touched there's a better probability its energy will help you feel more whole. As we have learned, what is truly holy is truly whole.

Some sacred sites carry historic religious significance. It might be a place like Capernaum, where prophets and spiritual teachers have walked and worshipped, or a place where miracles were conducted, healings and life-changing visions received, shamanic ceremonies enacted, and where shrines, temples, and cathedrals have been erected.

Some sacred sites bear striking geological formations such as Ulurru in Australia, the stunning snow-capped peak of Mt. Kailas in western Tibet, or a water spectacle like Victoria Falls in east Africa. Other sites might not bestow such powerful beauty. The heightened energy field might be less visible in places where it arises from subterranean mineral deposits, crystal caves, underground springs, or the confluence of geomagnetic currents.

What we've learned in our travels is that there are places sacred to the Earth where the soul of the planet surfaces in all its wholeness.

A sacred site is one where the Earth shows and goes to express its complete aliveness. One doesn't choose to live on a sacred site. One is invited to live there. [It is] a place where there are no statues or monuments, a place that carries and emits the light, life, and consciousness of the Earth, complete, ineffable, and mysterious.

Whether the area is sacred to people or the planet, the sad reality is that more and more are being exterminated, the radiant energy corrupted, gone.

Sacred sites are areas where dark forces seek to destroy, defile, and overburden. In many cases they have succeeded.

Valley of Death

One early evening, we walked to a Jerusalem park just west of the old city and gathered on a slope above a grassy basin. The Master informed us that our purpose at this site was to release the stuck souls of those who had been murdered there.

We have work to do. You have come here to give life to the beings that are here. They're not you. This is a gift. You are giving a gift, if you are willing. This is hell. You are sitting upon a hell. They died a horrible, cruel death in a belief system that said this was for their god. And they have been serving the god ever since. They have been waiting for those that would come to help release them — that were stronger than their gods.

There are thousands.

The part that connected their etheric souls with the human soul was entrapped because the deaths were so awful, or they were too enslaved by their god. So they were literally enslaved by a belief system [that told them to] keep believing the god is much more than them. Those souls don't reincarnate and they give nothing to the land. They give nothing to anybody.

The Master brought through an unidentified being who seemed to be one of the souls needing to be released.

UNNAMED BEING

Many, many eons ago this [place] carried many villages that were very dark and [the people] believed in human sacrifice. Small babies, young children, male and female, who were perfect of body and perfect of mind, were torched alive or [their] hearts [were] removed while [they were] alive and then thrown into the pits of fires with no ceremony and no one to weep except in secret for them. And women and men who were great sorcerers or seers were killed, [and] also midwives, healers, physicians, [and] scholars who could read the stars, who were knowledgeable. Does this still occur?

Those who were here were never mourned or grieved but [they] were told that this was to be, this was what god wanted, and they were supposed to smile in their agony. They made their agony a lie and made it good to be in agony, to agonize, to be in great pain. The sacrifice was good. This was, for many of you, your foundation of sacrificing. Even if you did not participate, these were much of the beginnings of how humans decayed, [and] that killed the soul of the body. The human soul was killed when the lies became truths.

The feeling I experienced being in the presence of so many stuck and traumatized souls was that of a thick, unmoving, heavy-hearted fog. We were tasked with releasing as many souls as possible. The Oracle's body served as the primary doorway through which the souls could pass as we put our attention on opening our hearts, sustaining a connection with each other, and running the figure 8 energy pattern.

The stuck souls of the murdered appeared to the Oracle as a colorless, dim mist. As she helped release them and reunite them with their higher selves, the once dull mist became infused with vivid, vibrant colors.

Releasing Souls

The method we've been taught to effectively release trapped or stuck souls requires open and unconditional caring with our hearts and our breath. We first seek to understand the common denominator that has fastened the souls to the site. This attachment can come from defeat on a battlefield, residual shock from a sudden death, a shared belief, or it might be an attraction to the prominent energy radiating from the place. The caring energy needed to help liberate the souls must be free of conditions and limitations, without the slightest hint of judgment or sympathetic grief. We're not looking for what we're going to get back. The gift is in the giving, sending caring energy to them with our breath. This heartfelt breath is like the wind in how it helps move the fixed energy, activate the souls, and open doorways for their release.

The next day at the Mount of Olives, a hillside east of the Old City, the Master informed us that many of the souls had been released.

It's a great blessing on all of you to do this for them. The more doors you open for others, the more will be opened for you.

Mt. Sinai Revisited

For this, our second visit to Mt. Sinai, it was essential the group be on the summit at sunrise, a time when the planetary alignments would be at their optimum for the work we were to do. This meant

Mt. Sinai Dawn

waking up at 3:00 a.m. to start the climb. Since I was feeling knots in my stomach at the hotel restaurant the evening we arrived (much like my previous experience in 1990) I opted, with my wife and a few others, to climb the mountain that night. So, we packed a bit of food, our bottles of Jordan River water, and some space blankets, and we hiked up with the intention of sleeping at the summit.

Our mistake was not taking a tip from the Bedouin cameleers, who sleep with their camels on the leeward side of the mountain where they are protected from the mountain's frigid winds. We walked right on past them in the night. Finding a fairly flat area near the top, we laid our bodies under space blankets to sleep, only to shiver the freezing night away when the wind kicked up. At one point in the middle of the night, I heard a scuffing sound and saw a fellow traveler's space blanket somersault across the rocky ground into the darkness.

We mustered in the chilly air of the summit as the first rays of the sun lit up the mountain range of jagged peaks and rumpled formations that looked like petrified clouds. The climb had been much easier for the Oracle this time because, "All the doors were open."

The Master welcomed us.

Do you know at this moment, at your Thanksgiving moment, [11-25-93] *that your planet is also lined up with its sisters and brothers, those other planets of the solar system, in an alignment of bringing spiritual energy into a physical formation?*

The Master brought in a planetary master, who led us through a ceremony with the water we'd brought from the Jordan River.

PLANETARY MASTER

Find the place of bonding with your planet that is your mother and father. And bond with the place in you that is the mother or the father — whatever body you may have. You must welcome the planet to the home of your body. And you must welcome your soul to the home of your body, the etheric soul.

The high places are the temples of the Earth. You will not desecrate them. In the caves are the wombs of the Earth. It is with the plains that you walk and learn to be a child, in the hills to be a young person, but it is [in] the mountains that you find maturity. It is there that the heart and the second chakra become as one. From this blending of the two, memories will come out of the light [etheric] soul with the human soul in the Earth, as it was before creation became so solid.

Can you begin to feel your hearts and your seconds [chakras] already blending? So I will ask you now, in the presence of the Earth, of your maturing, and your own mothering or fathering, to open up to the universe, to your solar system, and receive the planetary mothering and fathering energies.

Let those planets from your solar system combine with the energy of the Earth and the people on it; and touch those people on it that can receive it. At [this] moment the etheric is known to the physical; the physical is known to the etheric, and within the creation of the second chakra it is no longer inside, but is outside.

Jupiter reaches out with all of its grandeur and says. "I will make you more. I will expand you more." Saturn with its rings will bring the coolness of intellect so the brain may know both. Uranus will explode all doors open with laughter and joy. Pluto will make sure every detail is touched [and] nothing left undone, no stone unturned, every hidden secret touched. Mercury and Venus will bring the fire of the sun to this, for theirs is the sun. Neptune, the wise one, the holy one, will rain upon your soul water so as to make fluid that fire in the gut, so it doesn't burn you.

So beautiful are these planets. These are the ones aligning with you now. These are the ones most strong in alignment. And they've said to Earth, "And when will we be able to touch your creation? We have not touched those bodies that you have created. They must know of us. As they know of their own siblings, they must begin to know us more."

The Planetary Master then led us in pouring the water on our hands and bare feet.

PLANETARY MASTER

Repeat what I say before you pour water over your feet. Are you ready? [yes] You make me cold. [You make me cold.] That isn't quite what I was going to say. (!)

I pour this water over my feet to show my bonding of feet and planet; of human soul to Earth soul. As I pour this water I am bonded to all the solar system, sun and planets as to this planet. And not only will I bring in information as a body of this planet but as a body to all planets.

This water I wash with feet and hands will be of the oceans of all the universes. And let my heart be the connector to both, and bring the blood deep inside out to both feet and hands and acknowledge that the water comes from outside of self, and self must reach from inside out to receive the water and bring it in.

As we poured the cold Jordan River water on our hands and bare feet, we were to touch the purpose of our human soul and the purpose of our etheric soul, and to blend them together as best we could.

As we descended Mt. Sinai I asked my etheric and human souls to show me their purpose. I wanted it to be something grand, glorious, and relevant. What became immediately evident was how the mountain needed janitorial service in the form of picking up garbage and toilet paper left by years of tourists. Such neglect has a way of lowering the vibratory rate of a land. I happened across a crumpled gunnysack lying among the stones, so we filled it with litter and stuffed whatever else we could into our jacket pockets and backpacks.

The Teacher later pointed out how angry the sacred mountain was because of how it's been trashed and desecrated.

Landing

Over the course of every trip we'd be in constant flux, moving from site to site and lodging to lodging for two to three weeks with little or no time to process what we'd learned and embodied. We'd return home jet-lagged, sleep deprived, worn out, stretched and stuffed with new information, experiences, energies, and more questions than answers. After landing we'd need to downshift and re-integrate with who we were when we left, juggle back into daily routines, relationships, children, and chores. We'd return to our jobs reticent to share with fellow workers what we'd done on 'our vacation' knowing it might stir up judgment or create a rift. A number of the beings the Oracle had brought through on the trip would speak to us in forthcoming classes. Travel stories would be shared, the energy work addressed, discussed, and further explained. Those students unable to make the journey would receive the new information and the expansion of the soul work.

Months later we'd learn where the next adventure would take us, the librarian would pinpoint the sites on a map, and the preparations for our departure would begin again.

The Teacher's soul work is always evolving, yet it never drifts from seeking connection to all life with acceptance, caring, and honesty. We continue traveling to enrich our lives as we touch the spirit of other lands and cultures to discover more physical and etheric aspects of our selves, of the Earth, and the dimensions of its soul.

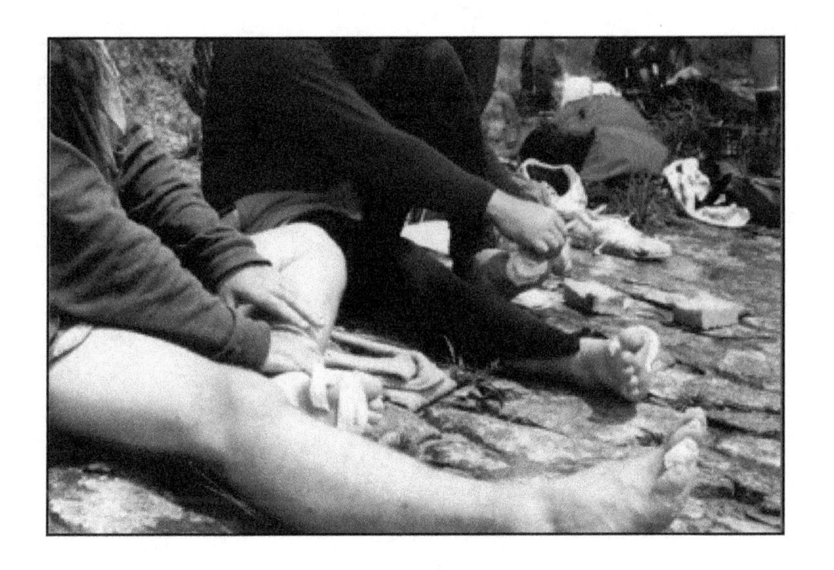

Epilogue

This book chronicles five trips in which members of a spiritual group traveled with the Earth Oracle to work with the first, second, third, and fourth chakras of the Earth. We have also traveled to many other regions of the world between and after the times of these journeys.

Join us on our *Travels with the Earth Oracle — Book Two.* It picks up where Book One left off with trips to the fifth chakra of the planet in the Middle East and the Gobi Desert, the sixth chakra at Lake Baikal in Siberia, and the seventh chakra in the Himalaya region of Bhutan.

For more information about the Earth Oracle,
and the soul-body blending work of the Teacher,
go to www.theearthoracle.com.

Appendix

Preparations for Departure

CARING

The Teacher would often speak about the act of caring, and how there was no end to it, no limit to the amount of caring a person can feel or give, because it is that deep.

Caring means that I care for you and I care for myself at the same time, simultaneously. It doesn't mean I care more about you [or] less about me. It's just I care about you and I care about me at the same time. And there are no measurements to it. You don't get fifty cents worth and I get seventy-five cents worth. It's not that I gave you seventy-five cents worth of caring, [so] you better give me back seventy-five cents worth. You cannot count or measure caring. Neither can you count kindness. And neither can you count compassion. And neither can you count forgiveness. And this is one of the reasons why when people are kind they never think, "Well, was that enough?" Much of your society is into counting and the measuring of things.

In order to actually have honesty, you must have caring. And it is that honest piece, that seeing piece, that knowing piece, that heartfelt piece done in caring with kindness and compassion and forgiveness that allows you to remove shame.

Caring can be done on a human level and a soul level. It moves on all dynamics, and that is why you will not be able to grow without it. You will only know how to be more solid and more small.

STRENGTH

This is the willingness to view your weaknesses, selfishness, narcissism, any of those darker pieces, in a more conscious, caring way. Ability is different than strength. Someone can be quite a capable person in many things, and quite talented, and yet not be able to know their darker pieces at all, or understand the impact on others. So we're talking about strength being the ability to see your impact on others, or care enough about others. We're not talking about body muscle, but heart muscle here. The strengthening of the heart. So that you can know your strength enough to know your darknesses.

DIMENSIONS AND DIMENSIONALITY

Planet Earth carries a dynamic kaleidoscope of dimensions. All the dimensions are essential. Nature does not waste. And given that they overlap, there is not a specific point where one dimension ends and another begins. Calling them dynamic is to emphasize their movement. The dimensions do not stand still. They can appear psychically like waves in constant motion, moving together. Certain features and life forms of the Earth exist in multiple dimensions, such as Mt. Roraima and the tepuis, the oceans, major rivers, and large fresh water lakes.

DIMENSIONS OF SELF

Expanding ourselves dimensionally is how we grow in consciousness and spirituality. Whereas one-dimensional people are flat and can only see the world the way they need it to be, multi-dimensional people are aware of the abundance of life that thrives on this planet. They can go outside of themselves to connect and experience a totally different life form, be it a whale, an oak tree, a river, or a dragonfly.

EXPERIENCING DIMENSIONS

Multi-dimensionality can be described as a place within a place within a place, where each dimension overlaps another and co-exists at different vibrational levels and time states within the same space.

Moving from one dimension to another is like walking across the sand into the depths of a beautiful ocean. It's easy when we first wade in. However, the deeper we go into that dimension the more we need to adapt to the changing currents we encounter. Each depth brings different life forms and different amounts of light and sound. We have to learn how to be with the changes in such a way that we are not harmed or lost, and we do not harm any other living thing along the way.

To move into another dimension is to experience it without control. This requires expanding your awareness and relating to the sounds you hear with your body, soul, and human soul connected. This is not a sound you hear with your ears; it's the vibrational energy you feel with your whole body and soul.

As you move through dimensions, your awareness is amplified. You become more sensitive to your surroundings. You can feel more vibrancy in the Earth and other life forms. Even the colors touch you. The Oracle said, "There is a sharing of self, spiritually and physically together. It is deeply intimate. There is no point of separation. You don't lose yourself, you become more. There's no loss here, only gain, and sharing, and learning."

As we experience other dimensions with our soul and body connected, we begin to touch different energies, and these energies might change how our body functions in the world. They can also open up parts of the brain that might then be used in new ways. The brain is not simply for thinking, it's also for dimensional expansion and experience. Many of the great inventions and science fiction stories have come from people who unknowingly went into another dimension and came back with an idea or vision, which they then manifested. This works both ways, in that people from other dimensions can enter ours and return with one of our creations.

It is rare to find a person who consciously moves in and out of dimensions. More often, the person is unaware they've floated in and out of another dimension. Sometimes it's as easy as setting a cup down, walking away, and coming back to find it no longer there. It's very possible the person was in another dimension when they set down the cup.

Human beings exist in different dimensions, as do other types of life forms the planet created to fit that particular time and space. These beings might not know we exist, just as we are unaware of their existence. However, what is happening in their dimension is not better or worse than what is happening in ours.

DIMENSIONAL GUARDIANS

The Oracle has expressed that, "As you consciously reach deeper dimensions, you will encounter guardians who serve as gatekeepers. These guardians are the embodiment of every living thing in each dimension. To pass into another dimension, you first have to notice the guardians are there. Then you need to give the guardians the correct sound in order to enter. This is not so much a password, but an equation you emit with your body and soul connected. It's not the dimension's job to understand you — it's for you to understand and match the dimension."

You might encounter a dimensional doorway between two trees in the forest or while hiking up a mountain trail. As you pass through the doorway, you might sense a shift in the energy and how beautiful the place is, but you won't receive the complete knowledge of the dimension without the guardians opening the door for you.

When you feel an openness, then you know you've walked through.

THE DEATH OF DIMENSIONS

Where the life force of the land is diminished or destroyed due to the destruction of forests, poisoning of waters, and/or extinction of species, the dimensions of the place might also be diminished, or irretrievably exterminated.

If you live or work in a place where this is happening, it will be very hard to remain emotionally and psychologically fit, and it will also be difficult to be creative there. In places where the life force is harmed, you might see a higher degree of deformities in children, a higher rate of cancer, and people who are more prone to violence and destructive acts.

The Amazon rainforest has been called the lungs of the planet because of the volume of essential oxygen it creates. However, in the last sixty years the burning and bulldozing of the rainforest has taken the lives of many creatures, medicinal plants, and insects that contribute to the aliveness of that immense area. It has also diminished the amount of oxygen circulating the planet. This destruction is akin to cutting a person's lungs out and asking them to breathe. But the tragedy doesn't stop there. The deforestation is also murdering the once-vibrant dimensions that existed there — and being so brutalized, the memory and time dimension of the forest is lost, and with it a library of invaluable knowledge we might have learned.

The energy meridians and ley lines that thread the Earth and serve as communication links with distant regions of the planet, as well as other worlds, are also impacted by our destructive activity. In places where there's a broken or damaged energy meridian or ley line, the ability of this planet to receive information from other life forms on other worlds is broken or disabled. A living planet cannot survive without the connection and energy that comes from outside itself. Much like a person who is disconnected or isolated, the more a planet is disconnected from the solar system, the less dimensions and aliveness it carries.

The destruction of the dimensions of our planet not only harms our lives and diminishes our ability to grow consciously and spiritually, it also imbalances other dimensions and unseen worlds beyond our awareness.

One of our lessons as human beings is how to be in these many dimensions and coexist with other living beings without looking to dominate or use them for our purposes. Rather, we must grow in consciousness by allowing the dimensions to change us. The Earth is our dimensional school. We might think we're the teachers, but actually we're students of the planet.

The American Southwest

HOW THE EARTH CREATES LIFE WITH SOUND

Sound is a primary creative energy on this planet. The Earth is a master composer of voices, mating calls, and songs in a wild variety of yaps, croaks, hoots, buzzings, barks, howls, chirps, yelps, roars, and clicks. Many sounds are beyond the hearing range of human ears — from the high, ultrasonic siren of katydids to the low-frequency infrasound of the African elephant. Audible or not, all these natural sounds contribute to the creative life force of the Earth, a life force that is weakened when a species is exterminated.

As a species dies off, naturally it is transformed into a more dimensional one with an increase in depth and range of touch. The Earth is able to create the new species using the sound of the one that is passing away. This sound-based metamorphosis is happening during the course of the extinction process while that species is still alive. The newly-evolved creature might not look like its predecessor, but it still carries the original tones and features of it inside. The ancestor's sound is part of its vibratory foundation. The transformation of dinosaurs into birds presents a vivid example of a natural extinction becoming a more adaptable species.

However, when a species is outright exterminated their sound is hushed from the world. Because the extinction happens so swiftly, the Earth is not given the regenerative time to transform the physical being into a new species from its sound base. Instead of a more conscious and evolved creature moving about the world, these untimely and unnatural extinctions create a void, a hole in the weave of life.

Since everything alive in nature is dependent on another for its existence, the extermination of one species not only eliminates the birth of new life, it also detrimentally impacts other creatures and vegetation that would benefit from its life, whether as a predator or as food. The murder of one deprives ten. Who knows what animal, fish, or insect is not in existence because of the extermination of the passenger pigeon, the great auk, or the Japanese sea lion.

With the increasing extermination of species, we are taking the very tools the planet needs to create and punching holes in the fabric of life. Holes in the ecosystem, holes in the food chain, holes where the air is sucked out of our lives. Connections are irretrievably lost and isolation spreads. Picture yourself needing a glass of water, but the glass is not there. You try to turn on the tap but your hands are gone. You kneel beside a stream to drink, only to realize your mouth has been erased.

By silencing species we are putting the Earth in a dysfunctional state where it cannot create in a way that supports its growth and the human beings who live on it. The planet grieves each loss deeply. It's like having your child murdered and losing the ability to bear more. The hopes and dreams you had for your offspring is now an empty space.

But there are things we can do. We can stop looking to make the world comfortable for us without first seeing the consequences of our actions. We can help restore the lives of endangered species. If they're allowed to continue living in their native environment, it will help sustain the lives of others. Zoos enslave creatures. The animals are unable to share their sound openly and completely. Studies have shown when caged wild animals are let back in the world and allowed to run free, they bloom.

Life can only go on living if it's allowed to sing.

Egypt

ABOUT BEAST

The beast follows the laws of the planet. It carries a physical dimension of karma. It also carries the level of planetary karma. Every living thing carries a level of karma from the entire planet. Karma is not bad or good. It's a term of living conditions. You're not frozen in it. It is not fate. It is not a cement road. It is a path every living thing must walk. Karma does not ask for sacrifice. It does not ask to be followed. It simply says, "You will walk it."

The beast inside your body very rarely resists karma because of the sense of WE. It will not try to deter it or try to change it in any way. It will walk with it. Join with it. It seeks the path of the WE. It expects to be touched by other living beings on this planet or even dead ones. It simply has no ability to know it any other way. It has total acceptance of this path of karma and that other living levels will touch it. Everything on this path will influence [everything else]. So you are never alone. That is the beast level of the WE. [The beast says]: "I'm an emotional instrument; I will respond to what touches me."

ABOUT THE LIFE-DEATH CYCLE

The Teacher has said that if we are not joining in the continuous cycle of life and death, we carry the separation of life and death inside us into the next world. That's why we keep coming back to bodies over and over.

Other beings have also spoken of this life-death cycle in different ways:

Living with life and death simultaneously is an ancient way of being. The energy of life and death together cannot be described in words or understood in words. Who you are is not important if you wish to move into this pure energy form.

Much of the learning has been lost except for people who live on the land and live with nature.

When murder is introduced to a planet on such a scale, the planet runs the risk of not being able to live with death and life. When this happens, planets become barren.

Venezuela

THE CAUSAL SELF

While there are parts of one's etheric soul that are formless, the causal self is one aspect that carries a connection with physical life. It is a very mathematical part that sets up how the soul will take on a physical body with the correct karmic connections, the parents and the birthing process. It also sets up goals and agreements for the soul and body to learn that lifetime. Souls are given choices, and are free to choose and learn from their choices.

The more life you experience, connect to, and embrace, the more you feed your causal self and it feeds you.

It collects the experience in the lifetime and looks at the balance and imbalance. When your body dies the causal self helps the soul embrace the physical life it was and allows it to bring in the karma. The causal self receives that information and keeps it. Those life experiences go to your oversoul.

Israel

CHRIST FORCE ENERGY

Christ Force Energy is not bound by any religion, or by humans. This quality of energy has been attributed to Jesus, yet every living thing can reach for it, integrate it, and learn from it.

According to the Teacher, a good example of someone in our time who has carried Christ Force energy is Nelson Mandela.

Someone with Christ Force Energy is looking to help strengthen the life-bearingness of the world around them. It's not about what is the right thing to do, it's about how life can grow. With Christ Force Energy you can walk in both life and death — allowing life and death to work together. You are connected with many different souls and an abundance of various kinds of life.

Glossary

Beast: An energy of the physical Earth that is carried in the human body from conception; located between the second and third chakra centers.

Chakras: Energy centers of the human anatomy. The Oracle sees them as lights. More information on chakras can be found in various books. Although differing attributes have been associated with the chakra system, the Teacher's work focuses on their basic functions:

> **First Chakra:** The Survivor. Base of spine. Provides the stability of the body in its needs and choices for survival. Brings energy from Earth and eighth chakra.
>
> **Second Chakra:** The Creator. Located in lower belly. Strong fire center of creation. Works with energy of Earth and first chakra.
>
> **Third Chakra:** The Integrator. Located in diaphragm area. Integrates physical and etheric energy into the body and how you bring yourself to your inner world. Helps integrate first and second chakras.
>
> **Fourth Chakra:** The Connector. Located in heart area. It is the integrator of the emotional body. It integrates all the chakras together.

Fifth Chakra: The Expressor. Located in the throat area. Integrates physical and etheric energy into how you present yourself to the world; what you bring to the world with your words.

Sixth Chakra: The Seer. The "spiritual eye" located in the forehead area. It is involved with the seventh chakra in intuition and soul sight, and it works with the inner ear for listening.

Seventh Chakra: The Soul. Located at the crown of the head. It is the connecting point for one's personal etheric soul and physical body. It connects to the genetic entity, and acts as a filter for the entry of soul energy into the body.

Eighth Chakra: The Earth. Located approximately 18" below the feet. It brings the planet's information about how to be physical into the body. It reflects what your body is doing, not what you are thinking. It has nothing to do with intention and everything to do with action. Along with the beast, this energy center is instrumental in filtering and regulating kundalini energy. To be grounded, this eighth chakra needs to be open.

Ninth Chakra: The Universe. Located approximately 18" above the head. Mostly etheric — serves as a filter for the entry of universal and etheric soul energy into the physical body.

Etheric Realm/Energy: It is like an ever-changing cloud, formless compared to the physical world, that carries a vast vault of knowledge beyond what we know.

Etheric Physicality: The Teacher's term for the blending of the etheric energy of the soul with the physical energy of the body where they come together in a mutually beneficial way.

Etheric Soul: One's personal soul, which is a particle of one's oversoul.

Figure 8: An energy pattern that is directed through the spiritual anatomy of the human body to bring balance to the body in a way that it can accept and blend with the etheric soul, the human body and the Earth.

Genetic Entity: An energy structure located in the neck area of the human body that serves as the body's link to the soul and carries the soul's information about the structure of the body in any lifetime.

God: The God of Many Names, the Godhead, the Supreme Being.

Grounding: The act of being anchored in your body and the Earth in present time — in your feet and behind your eyes. This can be done with exercises and visualizations to help open the eighth chakra. It helps to be in a place that is willing to connect back.

The Human Soul: A particle of the etheric soul of the Earth in the human body. In a sense, the human soul is what connects us to the spiritual Earth, while the beast connects us to the physical Earth. The human soul cannot exist without the beast. There is no separation.

I Am: The being state of the etheric soul, and all the many facets of the soul. A state that extends beyond self. Judgment takes you out of the I Am state.

Karma: The law of cause and effect. Negative karma can come as obstacles. Positive karma can give you a helpful boost.

Initiations: Experiences that open you and connect you to levels of energy that assist in your spiritual development. The success of an initiation is determined by how and if you choose to share the experience with the world.

Kundalini: A fiery Earth force (energy) that can activate consciousness in the human body.

Mediumship: The ability of a person to bring, through his or her physical body, the information and energies of non-physical beings and a variety of energy levels.

The Mother: A universal life-bearing and nurturing energy that instructs us how to be caring in actions and not just words.

Oversoul: One's etheric soul is a particle of the oversoul, which is a much greater soul.

Pyramid System: The three dimensional triangular system; one of the etheric energy structures of the body that serves the function of containing energy in the human body.

Running Energy: The practice of directing energy through and around one's body.

Silver Cord: The cord of life, made of thousands of energy strands, that connects the human etheric soul with the physical body.

Solidity: This is the Teacher's word for the lack of movement in the body, whether it is the inability to feel and express emotions, a lack of internal mobility, or a blockage that restricts the movement of energy. Physical fluidity is the opposite of solidity.

Soul Sight: The ability of the etheric soul to shed light (consciousness) on the shadowy, unconscious areas within the self and in the world. When you are connected with your etheric soul you are able to see and name things more clearly and articulate who you are and what you are doing.

Soul sight being that which removes all shadows from a darker point. It doesn't remove the dark point; it just removes the hiding places.

Soul sight brings with it the opportunity and the challenge to make new choices. There is an incredible responsibility that comes with increased consciousness. Failure to act on new awareness is akin to rejecting self and prevents further growth.

Soul Work: The term we use to describe the ongoing instruction, practice and learning experience of consciously blending our etheric souls with our bodies and with the soul and body of planet Earth.

Spiritual Anatomy: The infrastructure of the human body that guides, monitors, and exchanges energy with the etheric and the physical worlds. It consists of several subvisible structures including the chakras, the genetic entity, the silver cord, the pyramid system, kundalini, and the beast.

Spiritual Emergency: An identity crisis brought on by a sudden shift or mystical experience.

Tepui: The word comes from the language of the Pemon people, indigenous natives of South America, and translates to, "House of the Gods." It refers to the flat-topped mountains located in Venezuela and other parts of South America.

We: The state of the physical body in its connection to all humanity, planetary life forms, and nature.

Windows: In this context, a window refers to a situation, time, and/or place predetermined by the causal self, where a person's soul can choose whether to live on, or let the body pass away.

Acknowledgements

This work is not meant for the fanciful.
It is not work meant for the daydreamer.
It is meant for those who can rely on their own feet.

Ancient Earth Energy

Thanks to all the fellow travelers who participated in the trips and the soul work.

Thanks to all the audio recorders and transcribers, international guides and drivers.

Thanks to those who have helped in the writing of this book — in alphabetical order: Gretchen Alford, Elaine Anderson, Karen Anderson, Marc Anderson, Jane Ball, Justin Blum, Ken Brown, Renee Brown, Alta Engstrom, Patricia Hauser, Carol Hooker, Kathleen Kalil, Jedidiah Krauss, Jim Kreider, Verlaine Halvorson, Ami Ladd, Nellie Lochridge, Linda Logman, Dr. Michael Maley, Greg Miller, Betsy Nelson, Sally Nettleton, RoseAnne Roznowski, Veronica Smith, Denise Templeton, Jim Templeton, Carol Weber, and Pat Winkels.

I am deeply grateful to the Teacher, the Master, the Librarian, and the beings and spirits of the places we touched who continue to teach us how to live more conscious, soulful, and Earthful lives. I am deeply grateful to Donna Sarah Taylor, and to Lawrence Wade, Patti Landres, and Jessica Bryan for their insight and support through the many stages of the writing.

About the Author

M. Smith's geomantic work as an Earth energy practitioner evolved from his study and travels with the Earth Oracle. He is the founder of the Institute of Energy Arts (www.instituteofenergyarts.com), an organization dedicated to surveying and treating geopathic stress and other unhealthy radiations in the land. His projects range from clinics, to residences, schools, farms, restaurants, real estate developments, and corporate spaces. He gives lectures and workshops to health and wellness practitioners on Earth energies and the energy treatments he applies. He is the author of *A Year in the Field: Apprenticeship in the Energy Arts,* which can be read on the energy arts web site.

CPSIA information can be obtained
at www.ICGtesting.com
Printed in the USA
LVHW060910120819
627314LV00005B/287/P